"Low and Slow"

Fly and Fight Laos

Copyright © 2014-2016 William E. Platt

ISBN-10: 0692600868
ISBN-13: 978-0692600863
(HD images are available at this URL)
https://www.wep11345.com/book--low-and-slow-.html

Long Tieng flight line, 1969 O1, T28D, W. Platt collection

Table of Contents:

Dedication
Acknowledgments
Introduction
Forward

References:

Low and Slow website table of contents:
https://www.wep11345.com/book--low-and-slow-.html

Maps
https://www.wep11345.com/maps.html

Ray de Arrigunaga's "LAOS, The Secret War."

Part 1 Air Commando Journal Vol 3 Issue 1 pg 23

Part 2 Air Commando Journal Vol 3 Issue 3 pg 9

Part 3 Air Commando Journal Vol 3 Issue 4 pg 18

William E. Platt interview conducted by Maikou Xiong, Hmong TV, August 28, 2015

https://www.youtube.com/watch?v=t8fPMalMSRA&feature=player_embedded

Raven 43 interview "Eyes of the Attack" History Channel video, Suicide Missions,
 http://youtu.be/00YW1szygYc

Historical Material
http://www.t28trojanfoundation.com/secret-war-in-laos.html
http://content.time.com/time/specials/packages/article/0,28804,2101745_2102136_2102247,00.html

About The Author
https://www.wep11345.com/about-the-author-1.html

Dedication:

War is an ugly thing, but not the ugliest of things. The decayed and degraded state of moral and patriotic feeling which thinks that nothing is worth war is much worse. The person who has nothing for which he is willing to fight, nothing which is more important than his own personal safety, is a miserable creature and has no chance of being free unless made and kept so by the exertions of better men than himself. John Stewart Mill

We honor those special military and civilian personnel who volunteered their service, strength, resolve and blood to secure freedom for others. We cherish the memory of those heroes who laid down their lives for their friends. In the gloom of war's grief, we witnessed a greater love well beyond the call of duty.

Most citizen soldiers fight as patriots to serve and defend their nation's security interests. Other soldiers fight to reunite their divided country. Some fought because soldiering was the only work for pay available. They believed their leaders. What choice did they have?

Flawed treaties and superpower provocations generated the storm of conflict. The divided governments of Vietnam, Laos, and Cambodia fought their countrymen and neighbors in civil and regional wars for political power and economic control of resources. The separation of cultures was a way of life in SEA (South East Asia) where opposing governments, histories, religions, languages, and traditions produced many environments of bigotry, mistrust and the segregation.

The reasons for conflict may appear worthy and justifiable at first when the prize is intact and optimistically attainable. The price of war is destruction and grief. Leaders rarely estimate the inevitable costs before making the quicksand commitment to provoke and escalate the fight. Some false leaders promote and prolong conflict to amass personal wealth. In my eyes, they are war criminals. Even worse are the monsters who see war as a method to thin minority populations in their country. Others are willing to sacrifice millions of their citizens to achieve their national objectives. They will be judged.

A conservative estimate of soldiers and civilians killed in Southeast Asia's civil wars between 1962 and 1979 is 2,800,000 persons. Every life matters and every family suffered great loss. Future generations fear the legacy of terror beneath their feet. Battlefields laced with unexploded ordinance and environmental poisons were not the anticipated outcome of War. The land and people suffer the aftermath of terrible decisions.

There were Hmong, Lao Sung Meo, Khmu, Lao Theung, Lao Loum, Thai PARU, Khmer, mercenaries, American soldiers, airmen, CAS officers and many others who did what they thought was right at the time. We combatants did our best to win and believed our nations cause was our duty. As we witnessed the constant lies and betrayal of our values, many patriots lost confidence in our leaders' judgment and motives. They must be insane for the brutality was animal instinct gone evil. Brave allies mistakenly put their trust in our national resolve. As American causalities grew our citizenry rightly protested. Our political leadership cowered with desertion of other core principles. We soldiers felt empty leaving allies to fight and clean up the mess we escalated. At the same time, we were thankful that no more American lives would be lost. This was a "Catch 22" dichotomy of the first degree.

We still pray that our leaders would be wise and honorable in the future. In hindsight, fifty years later, we realize that our leaders did not learn from our wars gone sour. History repeats itself repeatedly. Hope remains that peace and sanity will guide our grandchildren's future.

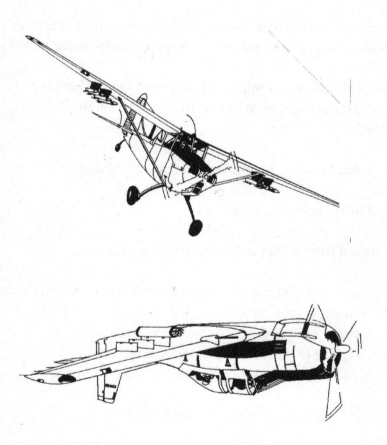

Acknowledgments:

We are thankful for our immigrant ancestors who chose the hardships and responsibilities of liberty.

We are blessed by creation and are so grateful for family, friends, country, and freedom.

We are excited about yesterday, today, and tomorrow; for Faith is the substance of things hoped for, the evidence of things not seen.

This book is dedicated to our improved understanding. "There is a spirit in man: and the inspiration of the Almighty giveth us understanding."

Thank you, Helen Murphy, for encouragement and editing assistance.
http://www.t28trojanfoundation.com/

Thank you Raven Briggs Diuguid for editing assistance.

Thank you Ravens' Jerry Greven, Smoky Green and John Garrity for the use of their photographic images.
https://www.wep11345.com/greven-collection.html.
https://www.wep11345.com/garrity-images.html
https://www.wep11345.com/greene-collection.html

Thank you, Lee Gossett, for the use of your images.

Introduction:

The quality of decision is like the well-timed swoop of a falcon that enables it to strike and destroy its a victim. Therefore, the good fighter will be terrible in his onset and prompt in his decision. - Sun Tzu "The Art of War."

Sun Tzu may never have dreamt of combat aircraft fighting in wars, but he understood the quality of the falcon's aerial skill applied to the warrior's way. To me, Will Platt is a Sun Tzu Warrior. He balances the inner spirit in the midst of a challenging war. Reflecting back on his tour of duty, Will focuses on his mission as a "Mike FAC" and then a "Raven" Forward Air Controller during an extraordinary moment in time known as the Secret War in Laos. His story is "Low and Slow," and he tells it with a free flowing writing style at times reminiscent of a songwriter with a lyrical simplicity yet complexity of emotions. His photographs depict a timelessness; although it has been over forty-five years, they are a priceless collection ranging from everyday life in Long Tieng to showing the ravages of war from above in his O-1 Bird Dog or AT-28D. He had the foresight to take many (unauthorized) photographs documenting what would otherwise be gone forever from memory. The year was 1969. It was the height of the build-up of the Vietnam War. Will was a strapping young man, in his physical prime as a pilot for the 5th Special Forces. In South Vietnam as an O-1 Forward Air Controller, Will happened upon two men who would change his destiny. He would strike up a conversation with two pilots who were talking about their flying and all the air strikes they were controlling "up country, across the fence." Intrigued and wanting to go where the action was, the two Raven's successfully recruited William E. Platt into their elite Steve Canyon Program. Raven 43, call sign "Tiny" was assigned Military Region II, the hotbed of General Vang Pao's war against the invading North Vietnamese Army and Pathet Lao. Long

Tieng or LS20A was home base; it was called the most secret place on earth because the war in Laos was highly classified, and the Raven's were there under covert operations. Will learned his enemies ways, he learned about the culture and beliefs of the innocent Hmong that he was defending, he knew the country's terrain and weather limitations but most of all he was one with his airplane. He called his air strikes like a well-timed swoop of a falcon with a deadly and terrible onset. He became Sun Tzu's Warrior; brave and smart. I will let Will finish his story; I know you will find reading his book captivating. I am humbled and honored to introduce you to "Low and Slow." Helen Murphy, T-28trojanfoundation

Iron sharpeneth iron; so a man sharpeneth the countenance of his friend.

Raven FAC , O 1, Rt. 6, Greven collection

Hmong warrior 1970, Garrity collection

In training 1970, Garrity collection

PDJ, Jars, PAVN bunkers 1970, W. Platt collection

Hmong refugees 1969, Gossett collection

Forward:

https://www.wep11345.com/book--low-and-slow-.html

This work is an expression of my experiences as a Raven Forward Air Controller during the secret war in Laos. My window of participation in that war was from December 1969 thru June 1970. The location was Long Tieng and the battlefield surrounding the Plaines De Jarres. The official history of American involvement in SEA has been well documented and is readily available online. The personal stories are still being written and published by the participants whose lives were twisted and tempered in the crucible of war. This work is about people I knew who risk their lives in a fight for the freedom of others.

This story has four threads that intertwine to weave a story cloth of hope and perseverance for war refugees.

The first thread is the universal struggle for respect, equality, and freedom that minority populations face when powerful enemies attack and oppress them.

The second thread is the unique character and determination of General Vang Pao, Hmong leaders, soldiers, and families at Long Tieng who stood strong to fight a gargantuan foe rather than submit to abuse and communist domination. "Give me liberty or give me death."

The third thread is a story about Low and Slow American pilots who volunteered to attack the beast and defend a very special ally. We fought to win while our government made treaties with Hanoi that did make war refugees of our homeless allies.

The last thread concerns the sheer magnitude of human suffering resulting from fraudulent treaties and political deceit. Our pathetic leaders abandoned loyal allies to communist power and vengeance. The eventual price exceeded two million dead.

What the young pilot meant to say... "If war is necessary and the cause is just, we must win quickly and permanently with minimum loss of allied lives."

This is a story of promise, betrayal, and hardship that progressed to a refugee gateway to compassion, freedom, education, and prosperity. The Hmong, Lao, Cambodian, Montagnard, and Vietnamese refugees from the Vietnam War produced vibrant communities in the United States. The Hmong persevered and learned to adapt to the American system without losing their cultural identity as Hmong or Americans. The American Hmong have cleared the path and set the example for new American pilgrims to follow.

Photographs are helpful in telling this story. Many images are included in this book while a larger collection is available by link to the author's secure website https://www.wep11345.com/book--low-and-slow-.html.
I hope this work is helpful to many in understanding the Raven's mission and mindset during the Secret War in Laos. This work may be encouraging for new to America immigrants whose journey here, like the Hmong, was filled with obstacles and suffering. The United States military veterans may find goodwill in stories of survival by faith and courage against great odds.

My memories are vivid; they shape my understanding of life, death, faith, freedom, oppression, and duty. In June 1969, I was off to Vietnam to save the world from the red tide of communist expansion in SEA.

In Vietnam, I was a USAF, 5th Special Forces, Mobile Strike Force, Forward Air Controller (FAC). My mission was to locate and destroy the enemy and his material. My flying skills developed with daily low-level aerial reconnaissance and Tactical Air Support for our Montagnard mobile strike force patrols. The Green Beret led, Special Forces A camps, Landing zones, (LZs) and Firebases near Duc Lop A239, and Bu Prang A236 were my green friendlies. "Mike 82" was my call sign. I flew over a vast, jungle and disputed border. The Viet Cong controlled all trails below the lush canopy. The People's Army of Vietnam, (PAVN) were dug in along the Cambodian border sanctuaries from mid-July 1969 thru December 1969.

Fire support bases (FSB) Kate, Susan, Annie, Helen, and Martha, were semi-fortified hilltop redoubts (Deep-dirt outposts with barbed-wire and trenches). They were mutually supporting artillery sites deep in the enemy controlled territory. I fought for their survival and helped in the evacuation of each FSB as the North Vietnamese Army (NVA) bombarded them from Cambodia and made direct assaults on the FSB perimeters. I went on patrol with the Mike Force strikers and experienced mortar attack, evasion, and ambush. In November 1969, I directed spooky gunships on targets from the sand-bag tower of A236. Sappers penetrated the wire beneath our flares but failed to reach the command bunker or ammunition storage area. My short experiences of ground combat reminded me why I joined the USAF and not the US Army.

Firebase Kate was within a few miles of major NVA's units. Kate was on a steep grassy hill and re-supplied by an air bridge of helicopters during good weather. Landing Zone (LZ) Kate was under siege by the NVA in the last days of October 1969. The weather for that week was low overcast ceilings and intermittent rain. There were American Green Berets, artillery officers, gunners, and a reinforced company of Montagnard strikers to defend the hill from a Regiment of the NVA regulars. Our men were running out of water, food, and ammunition. Our outposts were expendable in the eyes of the 23rd ARVN Generals who were in command of a full Division 25 miles away. Let the NVA close in on the firebase bait; then bomb them to destruction as they concentrate to attack. The 23rd Army of the Republic of Vietnam (ARVN) saw no reason to risk their forces to rescue or relieve a few beleaguered Americans and a bunch of troublesome Montagnard savages on an indefensible hilltop. Soon our firebase howitzers were destroyed, several helicopters were shot down, several re-supply, and aerial evacuation attempts were aborted. The helicopter rescue was turned back by heavy ground fire as I watched and listened in on their tactical frequency. The friendlies would have to fight their way to Bu Prang, at night, on foot, through six miles of NVA controlled forests. Most of our soldiers survived the gantlet. I was proud to have been a Forward Air Controller fighting to keep Montagnard strikers alive during those weeks of hard battle.

After a chance meeting with Raven Craig Morrison, I volunteered for the Steve Canyon Program in Laos. Quietly, I disappeared into a secret war of freedom fighters and their Controlled American Source (CAS) advisors in Laos. Long Tieng became my home, and the Hmong freedom fighters and Ravens became my family.

In Laos, I flew under the call sign "Raven 43". The beauty of the mountains could not hide a land full of war and sorrow. Freedom was the hope while persecution and dispersion was a reality. The Americans in Laos were all volunteers and experts in their specialties. The Hmong soldiers fought to defend their families and villages from an invading army of North Vietnamese communist soldiers and Pathet Lao (PL) irregulars. With family at risk, the Hmong soldiers were fierce fighters. Raven FACs at Long Tieng directed US airstrikes that served as General Vang Pao's versatile artillery. The defense of Hmong outposts was our priority. We disrupted the flow of enemy supplies and troops headed down the

Ho Chi Minh network of trails at every opportunity. We provided Close Air Support (CAS) for Hmong, Royal Laotian Army, and Thai units operating in our region. The Hmong endured discrimination and mistrust from Lowland Lao (Lao Loum), government officials, who feared an unpredictable armed force in the mountains north of the Mekong river. When Lao allies, the French, were defeated by the communist Viet-Minh in 1953, the Hmong continued to organize and fight for their leaders and a self-rule dream.

Here in Laos, the land belonged to the King and his princes. Ethnically diverse villages of various hill tribes were considered transient migrant communities by many Lao bureaucrats who had plans for the mountains, valleys, forests, and rivers. The Hmong leadership vowed loyalty to the King and the government. The government was administered by clan leaders, some with family ties to Thai Royalty.

Now armed and trained by Thai and US counterinsurgency employers, the Hmong posed a potential problem for Lao Loum clan political authority in the Xiang Khouang province and Vientiane. The Hmong dream of an autonomous province was reignited.

Courageously, the Hmong suffered increasing losses of young soldiers in the decade following the French defeat at Dien Bien Phu in 1953. In 1961, General Vang Pao and American CIA officer Bill Lair joined forces. Medical teams, rice, arms, training, air transport, and schools immediately improved the lives of Hmong people. The cost was young men turned soldier and sacrifice. As the confrontation with communist PL and PAVN units increased in northern Laos the evacuation of distant Meo settlements from combat zones to more secure encampment areas followed. Refugee men and boys took the only salaried work available to them; soldiering. Isolated refugee settlements and Special Guerilla Units became increasingly more dependent on USAID provisions of food, medicine, and necessities. Younger men were drafted into the irregular army as attrition spiraled beyond birth rates. The Lao Army and CIA then recruited fighters from the southern Provinces of Champaks, Salavan, and Savannakhet. They were organized into Special Guerilla Units (SGU). These mostly Lao Theung units from MRlll and MRlV would augment the Lao Sung Hmong SGU's in MRll when needed. Every year the war escalation increased as did the ethnic minority casualty rates. The Lao Loum losses remained proportionately low. The Lao pilots learned quickly and fought well.

Thailand viewed Laos as a buffer state between them and the Vietnamese. They had a stake in the continued viability and neutrality of Laos. Thailand sent para-military, border patrol, Police Aerial Resupply Unit (PARU) trainers, and military equipment to Laos. In 1969, more Thai pilots, T-28 fighter-bomber aircraft, and volunteer Thai artillery units arrived to support the Hmong resistance to communist forces in MRll. The fighting intensified until 1973 when we officially departed Laos, and beyond.

US advisors, suppliers, and transport providers decreased support due to another ill-conceived treaty with the North Vietnamese in 1973. We abandoned our allies to fight on with inadequate support. Within two years, the Royal Lao government fell to the communist factions who hunted down the remnant of American allies for extermination. After the fall of Long Tieng in 1975, and the fall of the Royal government, the Hmong and other Lao supporters of American policy were driven across the Mekong to Thailand. Many surviving Hmong fighters and families found meager existence within refugee camps there while they processed as war refugees for immigration to many foreign countries and cultures.

Eventually, some Hmong families became immigrants to welcoming countries including the USA. Immigration to America was delayed due to fears about Hmong traditions, shamanistic beliefs, and a history of opium cultivation and trade. Illiteracy, poverty, and language challenges could make assimilation in America extremely difficult. Those fears were overcome as the first Hmong to arrive in America adapted far more effectively than most believed possible. Despite the hardships of dislocation, assimilation, and social prejudice, the Hmong community persevered and now thrives. The Hmong now write their history and teach newly arrived immigrants and war refugees the lessons they learned in the process of adaptation to American life.

A remnant of Hmong forces remained an active insurgency for many years. They lived a life of escape and evasion in the dense forest and steep green mountains. Their mission was survival and armed resistance. Disrupting the communist government and military activity was a holding action until MacArthur returned to Manila. The remnant's vision was to topple the sitting communist government of Laos. Hmong never quit. Screw the detractors, skeptics, and cowards. Survive if you can, but, fight until your enemy is vanquished, or you die. It is a matter of ancestral honor and a hunter-warrior ethos. A warrior's commitment to his people, leaders, and mission is; Never give up. Never!

I will always remember and honor their steadfast opposition to a wave of communist domination as bitter as Mao's Red Guard revolution in China. Together we fought for freedom because we each understood that warriors fight rather than submit to tyranny, and injustice; Freedom is not free.

Hmong diligence and intelligence cleared a path up the education and economic mountain in the states where they settled. In a few generations of citizenship, Hmong-Americans have become respected civic leaders, teachers, and professional business entrepreneurs in their communities. They have grown in the American tradition without losing their unique Hmong culture. Having accomplished much, they have given back more. Elder

Hmong Americans, of my generation, have a love of freedom and understand the dangers of oppressive government. Too many of our children fail to embrace or respect the lessons we learned the hard way. We forgive them "for they know not what they do! Neither did we!

As for my family, we are thankful to count Hmong, Thai, Lao, Khmer, and a few Vietnamese, as neighbors. God Bless America!

Chapter 1

https://www.wep11345.com/chapter-1.html

Vientiane, US Embassy

All warfare is based on deception. Hence, when we can attack, we must seem unable; when using our forces, we must appear inactive; when we are near, we must make the enemy believe we are far away; when far away, we must make him believe we are near. -Sun Tzu "The Art of War."

T-28D, O1 Birddog, PDJ, Laos, 1970, W. Platt collection

Laotian Briefing for Military Region ll

At the American Embassy in Vientiane Laos, I met John Garrity, a civilian clothed, USAF Lt. Col. intelligence officer who was the Assistant Air Attaché. Obviously, John was the "old head" "been there, done that" center of knowledge and experience. He had seen more than his share of combat in Laos as a Butterfly FAC in 1966. I liked him from the first. We shared a very firm handshake as his eyes penetrated my character and resolve. He was not diplomatic, more straightforward opinionated, adamant, and persuasive to the point of indoctrinating. Then John became gentle, compassionate, and empathetic when he talked about the Meo (Hmong) mountain people we supported. John was a warrior, sidelined to the embassy but still fighting for the freedom, and the well-being of others. I readily absorbed the passionate speech of a professor. John was a captivating briefer; he understood and explained our military and political dilemma. His strength was not political correctness.

"This is the MRll situation," John said. I was paying attention.

"The Hmong culture and traditions are ancient Chinese mixed with adaptive traditions. They are hunter fighters, farmers, and survivors. The current military situation in Laos is dire. The next six months are critical. Airpower must win the day, every day. The Hmong are exhausted and depleted of fighting age soldiers." Soldiers from southern military regions are now augmenting Hmong guerilla battalions. Thai and Lao T-28 pilots and army units are now operating in the region to strengthen the resistance against the Pathet Lao and NVA advance during this dry season.

POLITICAL BRIEFING

"Ok son, here is what you need to know. There are Neutralists, Royalists and Communist factions maneuvering for control, influence, and power. There are plenty of corrupt players here with a mix of interests that revolved around the poppy crop and valuable mineral resources. The Mekong is a gateway to world markets. For many centuries, the black market trade in black tar opium has been the revenue stream that motivates the warlords, Princes, Kings and foreign powers. Morphine and heroin are produced locally and sold globally. For us, this is a simple war against Communism. For many others around this town, it is about wealth. There are minerals in the hills, fresh, clean waterpower in the mountains, and oil at the foot of the Mekong. Get the picture? Now, there is a good Prince, a bad Prince, and an unpredictable King. There are drug-dealing warlords allied with some Generals that run the military. Politicians are on the take. U.S. taxpayers pay the salaries of the Laotian military, government, and cronies. We provide food drops to hill tribe village elders who draft young soldiers to fight in the civil war. The Pathet Lao have Meo hill tribe fighters from distant provinces in their ranks that are trained by the PAVN army. Meo fighting Meo for money; who wins?

Now the Royalists are the King's men; the Neutralists are middle-of-the-fence sitters who have leaders loyal to both the King and the Communists. The Neutralists, do not want to fight anyone until they know who will win. The Neutralists pattern is to occupy a piece of the western PDJ around Mong Soui until challenged; then they run away from their semi-fortified positions at the sound of the first mortar round or sniper fire. The Communists move into a village for a few days and make a hasty retreat to the forest when allied air power arrives on the scene. All sides understand the dynamics. There is plenty of spoils for leaders but the young soldier bleeds and his family, and clan grieve. He fights hard for his relatives, leader, and self-respect.

The Pathet Lao tolerate the King for now but plan his overthrow eventually. He allows the Communist governors to manage the graft and pay him tribute. The Pathet Lao forces are paid, trained, supplied, and educated by the North Vietnamese. Some of their soldiers are recruited or pressed into service from other clans and tribes living on both sides of the northeastern Lao/ Vietnamese border. Their leaders serve the local PAVN army commanders who sway village leaders with bribes and promises of semi-autonomy, land, and resources when the war against foreign occupation is won.

They recite stories of the cruelty of colonial armies, the Chinese, Japanese, French, Russians, and now, Americans. "Let this be the last colonial power to kill your people," they said. "We will help you to a better life than the King of Laos will."

"Uncle Sam pays the salaries of most RLG politicians, generals, and Thai connections. The poor minority teenage soldier and their families have few life resources. Boys are drafted and paid to be soldiers in one army or another. This is Laos, "The Golden Triangle," where poor young men and girl's lives have always been a commodity. There are plenty of contractors and corrupt government officials vying for equipment, gifts, favors, and bribes from every source. Private interests, international spheres of influence, and un-enforceable treaties invited in this tragic war."

MISSION BRIEFING

"Military Region II will be your new area of operation. You will work for Joe Potter, who works for the Air Attaché, USAF Col. Robert Tyrrell; he works for Ambassador George Godley, who works for The Secretary of State, who works for the President of the United States. Know that the President has an eye on the Laotian part of this regional war. He recently said we do not have combat troops in Laos; only a few advisors, that is you. He said no Americans have died in combat in Laos. That is not accurate. Get used to it; deception is simply classified as Secret. Here, misinformation is public information provided by United States Information Service (USIS).

We are building the Lao Army and Airforce capability through our Military Assistance Program to prepare them for our future departure. This Kingdom is in for much more civil war when we leave." They are training to defend themselves, just like the South Vietnamese."

"We are all servants of our President and his State Department thinkers in DC. Ambassador Godley approves and directs the humanitarian and war resources in Laos. The SKY advises all including Lao Military commanders. Project 404 administers most DOD personnel requirements. We have a requirements office (RO) that matches needs with deliveries. Adaptive teamwork, common goals, and mission-dedicated individuals overcome the many challenges we face daily. Our mission requires us to advise, train, and adapt constantly. We must pool our resources, skills, and relationships to succeed here."

"Two priorities govern the application of airpower in Laos: (1) not to widen the war and risk Soviet, Chinese, or increased NVA involvement. The appearance of adherence to the Geneva Agreement is deemed necessary, and (2), we must prevent collateral damage and killing of innocent civilians. Any attacks against civilians are prohibited."

"There are major considerations when we design the Rules Of Engagement ("Romeos"). Foremost is input from the Lao Prime Minister, who had to say over where, when and how much airpower can be applied within the Kingdom of Laos. In most cases, Souvanna Phouma agrees with any Ambassador recommended operations or airstrikes as long as they are kept out of the news."

"Our involvement here has raised North Vietnamese costs to propagate this war and decreases the combat pressure on allied forces as we withdraw our military units from SEA."

"So far our efforts have been a qualified success. The goal of preserving the RLG's control of the populated Mekong Valley

Lowlands is being met." We anticipate that MRll, MR lll, and MR IV fighting will escalate before the spring wet season arrives.

"State Department, CIA, USAID, DOD, and USIS all contribute their expertise and resources to maintain and train the Lao Army and Airforce. This is their country, and they will eventually have to resolve their political differences with their neighbors."

"Skeptics, hawks, and doves monitor cable traffic from the U.S. Embassy. You are the tail of the dog and the tip of the spear at the same time. I hope you have some character because you and the other pilots are going to be making life and death decisions every day. Make us all proud and do what is right in your military mind. You will be held responsible for poor judgment that draws attention to our classified mission. Senior planners will shield themselves with the Rules of Engagement (ROEs) which change as needed to meet the tactical situation in the field. So, do what is right! If you are captured, provide only your name and USAID Forest service connection."

"You will be stationed at Long Tieng, 20 miles southwest of the Plaines des Jarres. Joe Potter is currently the Air Operations Center leader. Practically speaking, Joe is the Director of Operations, Maintenance, Supply, Morale, and Personnel. What he says, do! He is responsible for generating the combat sorties you get to fly. Men like Joe are Special Operation's best. They have proven they can accomplish our mission and solve problems successfully. Rely on Joe. Every senior pilot there is in training for his critical job. Watch him and learn. Joe is a perceptive Special Operations veteran. He coordinates directly with the top leadership at Long Tieng and this embassy. Never mention the CIA. Officers like Burr Smith and Jerry Daniels are the leaders of the SKY, Spooks, CAS (Classified American Source) officers. Substitute the term "Client," for CIA; they pay the bills, train, advise and coordinate the support for

General Vang Pao's tactical operations. Maj. General Vang Pao leads his SGUs and Cha Pao Khou pilots. He has the final say in committing troops in MRll. The Hmong T-28 Cha Pha Khao pilots are his to employ against targets of his discretion. The Lao and Thai T-28 pilots have a convoluted chain of command and strike targets determined by their leaders. They are less aggressive than the Hmong pilots who are dedicated and loyal to defend their families and relatives in the field. Our mission is to support General Vang Pao, and interdict the HCMT whenever possible. VP's fighters come from his loyal hill tribes and clans. He leads and fights by oriental standards of war and tradition, not ours. He shows loyalty to the Lao King and expects that the Hmong sacrifice will win respect and land of their own to administer. The Royalists have lost full control but settled for a three-party government structure. Lao had fought against the Chinese, Vietnamese, and Pathet Lao Communists constantly since WWII when they fought the Japanese. Violent Viet Minh border incursions followed the French Indochina War. The French, Russians, and now, the USA see this weak little country as important enough to spend treasure and men's lives to contain Communism and maintain a neutral government. This war supports the military-industrial-political interests of many countries. You can guess which ones."

"Use up, give away or sell the old military equipment so we can justify buying newer, more advanced weapons of war." Allied nations get our old equipment, and they pass their old equipment on to tribal irregulars." Everybody but dead fighters get something."

"The natural resources and geopolitical desires of powerful nations sway the immorality of it all. Without Vang Pao and his Hmong force, containing the western flank of North Vietnam, all could be lost. Right now, two crack PAVN divisions are held in place northeast of the PDJ waiting to re-take it. They maneuver to protect the communist supply lines to the south, but they really would like to control all of northern Laos. If they defeat Vang Pao at Long Tieng, many more enemy soldiers will be available to attack American forces attempting to depart SEA. Our Work is a holding action, but I doubt that General Vang Pao has been told that yet." His forces are weakened so more Thai augmentees, and Lao SGU's from MRlll and MR lV will soon be in route to Long Tieng.

Gen. Giap wants control of the PDJ, the airfields at Xieng Khouang and Mong Soui. Then when the time is right, it will be on to the Mekong, Cambodia, and eventually, Thailand. Many believe that is his goal and high priority. A Communist Thailand would be unacceptable."

Vang Pao's Special Guerrilla Unit (SGU) irregular army is the boots on the ground needed to hold territory. USAF and USN airpower is his long-range artillery. We currently have fighting positions on the ridgelines around the PDJ. Recoilless rifles, old French 75 and 105mm artillery pieces are still in use. You Ravens and our US fighter-bomber pilots will respond when VP calls for air power. You are the heavy weapon on scene. Expect troops in contact firefights while supporting road watch teams, and Lima Sites patrols. When you are not FAC-ing for VP, find valid targets of opportunity, and obtain clearance to strike from ABCCC or VP through Raven control. Clear the fighter-bombers HOT and get an accurate Bomb Damage Assessment (BDA) when the smoke clears if you are able. VP also has his AT-28D bombers. Their call sign is Cha Pao Khao. They operate out of L20A. They are very effective. Some volunteer Thai special units have 105 and 155 howitzer positions protecting the Long Tieng valley. Some Thai Special Forces units are on the PDJ as are RLA SGU's. FAN neutralists units currently hold Mong Soui. Your Intel officer, Joe Bauer, will debrief you daily. L20A aliases are Alternate, Channel 98, Home Plate, Karsts Central, Long Tieng, or Long Cheng. Do your best and do not get lost or killed."

INTELLIGENCE BRIEFING:

The first casualty when war comes is the truth.
H. Johnson

"We have air superiority, but you are within range of NVA Mig fighters flown by Russian and Vietnamese pilots. Check your SIX! ABCCC and radar should be able to provide advanced warning. Be advised we have not had incidents of shoulder-fired SA7 missiles here yet, but the NVA have been actively firing them at FAC's and fighters around the DMZ recently. That is a 400 hundred miles southeast of the here. The triple-A threat to you is very real; small arms, 12.7, 14.5, 23mm and 37mm AA, will target you. The NVA and Pathet Lao Gunners are well trained and experienced at ambushing low, slow airplanes. This target practice art form has been passed to the new gunner generations as a practiced skill. Their grandfathers, fathers, and uncles shot Japanese planes, French planes, and now our aircraft. The boys, who hunt birds with bows, arrows, slings, and stones, understand intercept, convergence, velocity, and timing. You are not bulletproof; neither are the fighter pilots you control during a strike. Know and respect your enemy. Out-think him. He has weaknesses, but you cannot outgun him every time. He will get angry, stay behind his gun and duel. He will focus to kill you to protect his people and assets. If there is a gun, it is protecting something."

"When a plane goes down a whole mess of pilots have to risk all in an attempt to save a brother. Enemy gunners have spider holes close to their guns. They are patient, clever, determined and willing to die for their cause or friends if necessary. If you are captured, you will be tortured and killed. So far, very few prisoners have been taken and kept alive for very long in Laos. Atrocities, ethnic cleansing, and re-population of conquered territories with loyal meo or Vietnamese citizens are normal events for the Communists. Remember the cold-blooded murder of 5000 civilians at Hue during TET 68. That is the typical brutality of Asian war."

"Here is your passport. You are now a civilian contractor, a USAID forest ranger, doing Timber surveys in northern Laos. Got it? That is your cover story. Stick to it! You are no doubt a truthful, officer who now is going to have to live a lie. Sun Tzu said, "War is the art of deception" You are not here; you never were here. You are in the black and Uncle Sam may not come to your rescue.

"Have you read Sun Tzu, studied Confucius, or Buddhism?"

"No Sir, not yet," I admitted.

John gave me pamphlets on several Asian master teachers.

"Know your enemy," he said in a serious tone.

Next, Col. Garrity showed me a film on the history and struggle of the Mao peoples over the centuries. He told of the vengeful razing of ethnic villages by the communists.

"Enemies came from all quadrants. There were Chinese, Siamese, Khmer, and Burmese raiders and frequent Vietnamese attacks. The rouged jungles and steep mountains provided hiding places, defensible high ground, and sanctuary for the mountain tribes and clans. There are many one-lane dirt roads on the PDJ, but in the mountains, there are just trails through the sharp and steep, karst formations. Natural migratory footpaths, hidden valleys, fresh, clear mountain springs, and streams link habitable caves and outposts. Before modern weapons arrived, spears, crossbows, snares, and pits kept invaders at bay. The Hmong have no written language; only oral traditions passed on by elders, shaman on embroidered story cloths. Some Meo (Hmong) speak and write a little French; most do not. Schools are very scarce, and libraries are nonexistent in the vast rural areas. There are over fifty different dialects spoken by hundreds of semi-autonomous clan settlements. The up-country Pathet Lao Communist soldiers are often of Vietnamese descent; most are Meo not allied with General Vang Pao. Non-allied clans and villages are caught between the warring factions. Tens of language variations are used. There is a historic wealth of bad blood between many of the indigenous villages and clans. Many village leaders want to remain neutral. They were compelled to take sides. Settlements are pressured to serve the needs of either, or both combatants as it became expedient to survival. They submit and do what the man with the gun tells them to do. All are in fear and subjection with nowhere to run or hide. Pease negotiations failed. Now there is this bloody war for political and military control of this region. The King claims it, the Pathet Lao want it, and the Hmong tribes expect autonomy. The Vietnamese want to manage the resources, and the Thai government wants a Lao buffer to their border. The Chinese want a friendly communist neighbor, trade, and natural resources. All the ordinary people want is a peaceful place to live."

"The lowland Laotians along the Mekong River valley, he said, too often demean the Meo for their cultural peculiarities and lack of sophistication. The Lao Sung have shamanistic belief, and the influences of their heritage include teachings of Buddhism, Taoism, and many-other-isms. Written language skills are "stick in the dirt" drawings. Lowland Lao often treat the Meo as rednecks treat ethnic minorities in the U.S. These indigenous Hmong people are proud and wanting freedom from oppression. They can be fierce fighters, but they would prefer farming, family and a taste of opium. The Hmong clans in Long Tieng love General Vang Pao. He is a hero and protector of the major allied clans. He inspires courage and determination with a strong grip and shows no mercy for enemy or turncoats. His tenacity and clan blood have, until now, withstood permanent Pathet Lao and PAVN occupation of their sacred mountains around the PDJ."

"During the last three months, we have overrun NVA and Pathet Lao positions on the PDJ. Our helicopters carry Hmong troops to mountaintop ridgeline fighting positions. We dig in and build dirt fortifications overlooking the PDJ below. Helicopters and airdrops from contractors Air America and Continental Air service accomplish re-supply. The NVA will counter-attack as soon as the dry season has hardened the roads and trails. So Mister Forest Ranger, be smart, be elusive in the air, be alert on the ground. Find enemy targets and destroy his materials and troops. Demoralize him, as he will attempt to do to you. Do your best to stop the flow of equipment and supplies headed south along the trail. Protect the friendly villages and the General's hilltop positions. That is your mission."

"Any Questions so far?"

"No Sir!"

"Lt. Platt, I understand you were a 5th Special Forces Mike FAC in II Corps. Challenging duty? he asked."

"Very intense Sir."

"Your experience defending A camps 236 and 239 this past fall should serve you well. Did all of the camp logistical support have to be flown in by Helicopter?"

"Yes, Sir."

"As the NVA travel his supply lines stretched thin and his vulnerabilities increase. We cut and slow those lines at every opportunity. Defeating him in southern Laos and Cambodia may be the future strategy. Plans change daily as dictated from Washington DC. Henry Kissinger is negotiating peace with master deceivers in Paris. Vietnamization, the withdrawal of our air assets, and the bombing halts of the North may well doom our allies. Extermination of all who fought against the Pathet Lao and PAVN is likely based on norms of Asian war. No one will come to the rescue if we lose the war by treaty or quit."

"That is the lay of the land Mister. Any more questions ask the other Ravens for a brief when you get to LS 20A. Be careful son; this is dangerous territory, big guns, bad adversaries, and no one takes prisoners. You are always behind enemy lines. They want to kill you, and they will be shooting at you every time it is to their advantage to do so. You will find yourself in the company of America's finest FAC's and Special Operators. Be creative and read Sun Tzu? We are men of integrity and discipline, but this war is not moral, truthful, or just. Mixing truth and lies with reality and near death can mess with your mind. When you return to Vientiane, come by the Embassy for a chat. I want to hear how you are doing. Good Luck."

"Thanks, John."

PDJ Rice, 1970, Garrity collection

O1, Fuel, rockets, PDJ, 1969, Garrity collection

Chapter 2
https://www.wep11345.com/chapter-1.html

Raven Leaders at LS 20A December 1969

There is no instance of a nation benefiting from prolonged warfare.
-Sun Tzu

Joe W. Potter, AOC, 1969

Joe W. Potter was the Air Operations Center (AOC) leader when I arrived in Long Tieng in December 1969. He was a well-liked and respected by his troops. Joe was a seasoned, special operator with the ability to keep airplanes flying in a primitive forward location. Joe would improvise as needed to fly and fight. He rotated back to the U.S. in early January, and Jerry Rhein replaced him in that critically responsible position. The AOC job description was to generate combat sorties for General Vang Pao's air power and airborne artillery needs.

Long Tieng, Skyline Ridge, 1970, W. Platt collection

A1 napalm strike, Rt. 6 1969, Greven collection

Raven, 01 Chief FAC

Bob Foster arrived in Vientiane in early January 1970 and became our "Chief" Raven FAC. He flew into Long Tieng as the pilot in command of an RLAF U17B. He greeted the team as a good coach would and announced that he was stationed in Vientiane with a mission to keep the monkeys off the back of the Ravens.

"Do your job well! Go free the oppressed!" he said.

Bob Foster was a full colonel in a Thai-tailored, dark blue flight jacket with matching throwers and stylish black Italian pull-on boots. His outfit featured zippered bicep pockets on both sleeves and map pockets below the knees. He wore a sidearm that may have been a Colt 44 revolver. A CAR-15 was strapped across his broad shoulders. Bob had the credentials of an experienced Forward Air Controller. He also was our cool operator presence and voice at the US embassy. No one would besmirch a Raven while he was in the briefing room and we were in the field. Bob had social officer skills. He got the "word" direct from the Ambassador, and Air Attaché after hours, socially. Bob was on the inner circle militarily, para-militarily, politically and socially. He represented Ravens and took responsibility for our brash combat mode repeatedly. He was our shield from what flowed downhill from blame-game administrative failures. On the social level, he and his wife befriended RLAF Generals and senior aviation peers. The man was smooth in a courteous, warrior's way. Bob Foster and his lovely wife Jinx moved into a comfortable villa near the U.S. Embassy where farewell and welcoming parties were enjoyed by the Ravens and the 404 Air Attaché team. He flew to each of the forward locations to evaluate conditions and morale. He appreciated our tireless diligence. Bob's responsibilities did not include flying into battle leading the fight. That responsibility would fall to steely-eyed Captains and fiery Lieutenants. Bob Foster was often the intermediary between frustrated AIRA and 7/13 Air force planners and the operators.

In the air, the Raven team was all-professional. On the ground, booze, the medication of choice, brought out demons in many of us. Inappropriate behavior was a part of the warrior culture; for tomorrow, we may die. I was fortunate to usually fall asleep after a beer or three with the 404 team after dinner. My survival depended on being alert, fresh, and airborne before first light. How to let off steam, and come down off adrenalin after a long day's fight was a personal choice and varied with our personalities. We were a feisty gaggle of aviators.

My roommate at Long Tieng was Craig Morrison. We usually spent the mid-evening hours reading and writing home to wives and family. Habitually we turned in early and were wide-eyed and bushy-tailed in the wee hours of the dawn, ready to fly and fight, fresh, sober and alert. First light weather patrol was always beautiful and peaceful in a mysterious way unlike the furor to come later in the day. The mist on the mountains, the color of a rising sun, there was peace, and calm for a few mesmerizing moments over the land of a million happy elephants. Suddenly, breaking the silence and tranquil mood came a desperate call for a Raven; today's war has just begun. Push 'em up; set 'em up, engine and guns ready to rumble. Let us do this.

Rt. 6 Road cut, interdiction HCMT, W. Platt collection

The AOC (Air Operations Center, Commander)

Jerry Rhein was a "get it done right" kind of man. He was a man of few, but serious, poignant words. I can hear him now "OK, what did you learn from that?" An old school, no BS, USAF propeller head, fighter pilot, instructor pilot, and flight examiner. He was born to fly and train less experienced men to survive in a danger-filled profession of fighter aircraft, bombs, guns, and aggressive personalities. He was a serious special operator who commanded our total respect. No one crossed him. General Vang Pao trusted and protected Jerry when a downtowner wanted him thrown out of the country for flying with the Cha Pao Khou. Jerry Rhein was the consummate trainer and teacher. The Hmong pilots benefited from his vast AT28 experience and prudent counsel. Jerry was always in charge, and his team worked hard to do the mission his way because it worked. Jerry was a "sensei" of air to mud combat. There was Jerry's way and the wrong way. We listened to him and learned what he expected from us. Jerry Rhein taught us to be in control of the storm.

I share Jerry's Biography as an example of the experienced Commandos who led the Ravens to war.

Maj. Jerry Rhein AOC January 1970, 1972, 1973

Jerry Rhein was born on March 20, 1933, in Vineland, New Jersey. He attended Miami University in Oxford Ohio, for two years before enlisting in the Aviation Cadet Program of the U.S. Air Force in December 1953. I was eight years old. He was commissioned a second Lt and awarded his pilot wings at Waco, Texas, in March 1955.

After completing Interceptor training, he served as a fighter pilot in West Germany in 1955. Lt. Rhein completed F-84 and F-100 Super Combat Crew Training, and Instructor Pilot School. He was an

Instrument Instructor Pilot with the 831st Operations Squadron at George AFB, California. In 1962, Jerry was assigned as a Forward Air Controller (FAC) with the second Air Division at Tan Son Nhut AB, South Vietnam. Next Jerry trained pilots in the T-28 Trojan and U-10 with the 319th Troop Carrier Squadron Commandos, at Hulbert Field, Florida. Capt. Rhein then served as an A-1 Sky Raider instructor pilot at Hulbert Field. In 1966, he deployed to Southeast Asia for a 2nd tour of combat duty as an A-1 pilot with the 1131st U.S. Air Force Special Activity Squadron at Tan Son Nhut AB, South Vietnam. Next, he was Chief of the Fighter Branch at Headquarters U.S. Air Force Special Air Warfare Center at Eglin AFB, Florida followed by more A-1 and T-28D instructor duty at Hulbert Field.

I first met Maj. Rhein in December January 1970. He was my new AOC commander at Long Tieng. He was a problem solver and superior leader who let us do our work without tight supervision. He rotated back to the US in June 1970, when did I.

In November 1970, Jerry was the A-1 Sky Raider lead pilot for the Son Tay Raiders. They were sent to rescue American Prisoners of War held in North Vietnam near Hanoi. His gallantry and mastery of nighttime, blacked out, tactics for protecting the rescue team soldiers on the ground saved many lives and earned him a silver star for valor.

He flew with distinction and trained hundreds of less experienced pilots to fly and survive in the hot zone. Promotions were not his primary goal. Do the right thing regardless of the career consequences. He volunteered again for SEA duty and deployed for his fourth tour as an AT-28D instructor pilot with the 4407th CCTS. He then served as the Commander of the MRlll Air Operations Center in Laos until 1973. His final assignment was in Stan/Eval as a flight examiner with the first Special Operations Wing at Hulbert Field until his retirement from the Air Force in December 1973.

After retiring from the Air Force, Jerry flew as a civilian pilot for Bird Air, Britt Airways, and as a corporate pilot. He served as a volunteer with the Okaloosa County Sheriff's Department in Okaloosa County, Florida until his death in February 2010.

His Silver Star Citation reads: Major Edwin J. Rhein, Jr., distinguished himself by gallantry in connection with military operations against an armed enemy of the United States during the Prisoner of War search and rescue operation at Son Tay, North Vietnam, on 21 November 1970. On that date, as an aircraft commander of a flight of attack aircraft providing close air support for the rescue ground forces. Major Rhein, with complete disregard for his personal safety, and in the face of intense enemy ground fire, anti-aircraft artillery, and surface-to-air missile fire, repeatedly led his flight against enemy ground forces attempting to engage the rescue party. Because of his leadership under fire, enemy reinforcement efforts were very unsuccessful, and the rescue force was able to complete the mission without a casualty.

Jerry was a great commando pilot, an outstanding friend, and the real leader of Project 404 and Raven FAC operations while I was in MRll.

Chapter 3

https://www.wep11345.com/chapter-3.html

Ten soldiers wisely led will beat a hundred without a head.
-Euripides

PDJ Orientation Flight

Craig Morrison, L20A, 1969, W. Platt collection

My roommate of several days, D. Craig Morrison handed me a checklist and spare flight helmet.

"Johnnie is our crew chief; he will help you strap into this Tango and get your communications wired hot. Read me the checklist, and I will respond with what I am looking for in the cockpit. Familiarize yourself with the EMERGENCY procedures and pay special attention to the Yankee Extraction System Warnings, Cautions, and

Notes before we take off. I will motor mouth as we go so you hear the what, why, and therefore of my experience and reasoning."

He did as promised.

"Arming pins pulled." "Lord keep us safe, in Jesus' name." "Cleared for takeoff. Every climb out is maximum performance. We need to know how the bird is running today. If we are going to have a problem, let us have it here and now rather than when we are deep in NVA territory. Gear up, Flaps 10 and L/D max to level off. At our weight, temperature, and density altitude we should climb at almost 2000 ft/min. Survey the weather, cloud bases, wind direction, and velocity. Remember the way home and always leave yourself a plan and fuel to get home regardless of the weather. When the mountain wind blows, expect strong downdrafts on the mountain's leeward side and strong lift on the windward side. Canyons and valleys can be "knocking you down" turbulent. Radio transmissions are by "line of sight" so below the ridgelines flight communication are unreliable. Keep the common Raven radio net updated on your location and intentions. On our left is the back door to Long Tieng from the PDJ. The Nan Ngum river flows from the northern PDJ, through mountain gorges back south within 8 miles of Long Tieng. Fly it low in good weather, so you feel comfortable when the clouds put you in the tunnel below the ridgelines. When the bases of the clouds are below the ridgelines to the east of 20A, and it is impossible to squeeze through the "Hump" without going IFR, then the back door Nan Ngum River is an option. On our left is Mong Soui. The RLA Neutralist garrisons hold the airfield there at LS 108 now, but Communists re-take it several times a year. Mong Soui was a neutralist stronghold before our About Face campaign last fall. The RTAF and RLAF T-28 pilots fly combat sorties from Mong Soui now. We will now fly east along Route 7 looking for recent activity.

AAA, PDJ, W. Platt collection

Notice the bombed-out 37mm anti-aircraft gun positions on our left just north of the road. It is in the shape of a ring with a mix of 14.5mm weapons protecting the larger, slow tracking 37mm anti-aircraft weapons. Notices in the tree line are deep bunkers. There are several NVA batteries like this along the northern PDJ. Notice the new camouflage and freshly dug spider holes near the guns for crew shelter. This site is active today. If you see smoke or flashes, they are shooting at us. We will report the coordinates and our observations to Cricket our EC-130 Airborne Command and Control Center. They represent the 7/13th Commander. They will coordinate a night strike on those guns. Notice the unconcealed truck north of the ring. Striking now, below the clouds, would give them a distinct advantage against our fighters. Without radar, they will be very vulnerable to attack at night. Cricket will order up an ordinance load for our fighters that will destroy the weapons, supplies, and bunkers for a few days. The NVA will repair our damage within a week. The NVA will have an ammo storage area within 50 yards of the guns and a ready supply of shells in bunkers closer to the gun. There will be a crew bivouac area in the trees, along the stream to the north and under the thickest canopy. Notice the large caves. The NVA are moles. We could strike now, but the weather would force the fighters to drop their load from a very low altitude and dive angle. Exposing our pilots to concentrated fire during daylight is unnecessary unless our ground force is threatened. This AA battery is not going anywhere. The night fighters will saturate the area when the weather clears, and the conditions do not favor the gunners. Cricket will warn all friendly aircraft of the reactivation of this threat. Moonbeam will relieve Cricket and take over command and control of night strikes. Post-strike RF-4s will photograph the results for a Bomb damage assessment to determine if another strike is needed to shut these guns down. We are coming up on Khang Khay. Those white buildings are the Chinese Cultural Center. They are full of NVA supplies. A half mile east is a lovely Buddhist Temple surrounded by military equipment stockpiles. We cannot strike within 500 yards of those buildings according to the current Rules Of Engagement. Road Runner Lake is a prominent landmark and saturated with AAA. The inbound fighters can see it from 20 miles away, so we use it as a rendezvous location for the fighters when we have good visibility. In marginal weather conditions, we use radial and DME off of Tacan channel 98. That navigation aid is located on Skyline Ridge above L 20A near the ADF beacon.

As the fighter formations approach the rendezvous point, we pick them up visually, give them a heading, and distance to the target. Complete the target briefing to include the threats they can expect to encounter and the best bailout heading if they take hits and need to eject. Here in northern Laos, the fighters can always expect small arms fire or heavier AA on their run into the target."

Craig rolled in hot from a half a mile away and 3500 ft AGL. He fired off a volley of 14 high explosive 2.75-inch rockets into a thick canopy just north of Route 7 in the free-fire zone. Just as he predicted, muzzle flashes and gray smoke erupted from a concealed gun ring nearby. Again, no Fighters were available. "Time to depart the area. We have burned half of our fuel, so we reconnoitered back up the valley's western slopes and expended seven of our remaining 14 WP rockets in areas where active trails ended in the heavy canopy and small streams intersected the mountain bases at the valley floor. We will make one more low circle around our Phon Nok Kok outpost to clear their perimeter." We expended our remaining rockets on likely enemy observation posts within a half mile of our Hmong force outpost on Pnon Nok Kok Mountain. Notice the troops cheering from their foxholes. Ok, low on fuel now."

SGU outpost, Greven collection

We worked our way back west along Route 7 to Lima Site 22 near Xieng Khouang and landed the T-28 without incident.

PDJ, LS 22, refuel and rockets, W. Platt collection

Craig and I built up our new rocket load by screwing warheads into rocket tubes, setting the fins, and pinning the motors in the rocket launch tubes. Nung mercenaries refueled the bird while we opened our spaghetti meals ready to eat. Needing a leg stretch and a can of soda to wash down the MREs', we ventured into a holding area where 10's of captured enemy heavy artillery pieces and many PT-76 tanks were lined up; spoils of the About Face NVA sweep last fall. We took some photos, climbed in and around the undamaged equipment and walked back to our T-28 for another mission. Craig gave me a quick history of the About Face helicopter leapfrog assault across the PDJ. The NVA had abandoned supplies and equipment and scurried for their lives back to the relative safety of the Ban Ban valley to regroup. They did not have the time to destroy the equipment before making a getaway.

PDJ, tanks, mobile twin 12.5 AAA machineguns, Greven collection

That night PAVN sappers got inside the wire of LS 22 and destroyed each gun and tank with grenades so they could not be used against their forces.

Back in the T-28, weapons loaded and aircraft topped off with 100-octane fuel from 55-gallon drums, we received a call requesting Raven help. We took off and headed southeast toward Muang Koun. Craig requested fighters and soon had two flights of two A-1Es' headed for a rendezvous. An outpost was taking mortar fire. The site sat on the top of a ridgeline; it was 75 yards long and 40 yards wide. The Hmong fighters were dug into the high karsts and had a near vertical drop on two sides and thin steep ridges on the other two.

Greven collection

We arrived on scene and orbited looking for the enemy mortar on the slope below. It is 1400 hours, and the weather is deteriorating. The southwesterly wind was strong, gusts and turbulent were heavy from the 7000' mountains directly upwind a mile. The cloud bases were 1500' above the ridgeline compound at 5000'. The valley below was about 3300'. The sky was dark, overcast, threatening, and menacingly beautiful. Here I am in the back seat of an AT-28D, with a friend and great pilot up front making the strike decisions. The situation was this: the mortar rounds began impacting in and around the site perimeter an hour ago as the weather had become overcast. They were expecting a major assault at dusk. They asked for air strikes 75 yards southeast where the clear-cut brush meets the tree line. "Please hurry Raven."

Two flights of A-1's loaded with cluster bomb units (CBU), 500 lb bombs, and 20mm cannons came up on the radio and checked in.

We copied the fighters' weapons load, and Craig's strike briefing went something like this.

"Hobo 31 lead this is Raven 49. LS 103 is Troops in Contact (TIC) with the enemy 100 yards southwest of their ridgeline position. Yellow smoke is the friendly position; the white smoke is the target. Your Raven will be in a random orbit southwest of the target below 5500' mean sea level. I will keep you insight and stay clear. You will be cleared random headings and multiple passes at your discretion. Anticipate small arms and 14.5mm guns with tracers during your strike and exit. Best bailout heading is west-northwest for 20 miles over the PDJ. Understand you are 040 at 35miles off the Ch 98 Tacan station at 12,000' I will pop up through the clouds to 11,000'. Call visual over."

Craig transitioned to the instruments and entered a level climb into the overcast. Two minutes later, we popped out on top of one deck at 9000', and were below another scattered layer at 13,500'. We entered an orbit and spotted the fighters. They rejoined with us in close-trail formation. We started down through the soup and broke out in the clear and broke right toward the target; 2 o'clock at 4 miles. The friendlies popped a yellow smoke, and Craig rolled in, fired a WP Rocket 100 yards southwest, and immediately cleared the A-1's hot. Lead rolled in and laid down CBU while #2 followed from a slightly different heading covering lead's delivery and dropping more CBU. We could see the flashes as the cluster bombs (CBU 14) impact was on target. The Lima site radio operator confirmed the first pass was on accurate and not too close to their forward position. The A-1's continued making passes until all they had left was 20mm cannon. To this point, we had not spotted any ground fire although the A-1's had spotted scattered spider holes and a few makeshift bunkers in the strike zone. They held high as Craig dropped down to ridge level for an assessment of the strike effectiveness. We got a good look and banked hard right over the target area.

As we initiated the pulled up, a 12.5 anti-aircraft machine gun opened up from adjoining karsts 200 yards south of the first target and a third of the way down the sharp embankment. Tracers were flying by as I calmly said "Duck" into the microphone. Craig was already crouched low in his seat as a round went through the cowl and slammed into a cylinder push rod and severed an oil line with a sound and jolt of impact never to be forgotten. Instantly the windscreen was covered in black oil, and the engine vibration was violent. We were below distant ridgelines, almost out of airspeed, 900 feet above the valley floor and descending. Within seconds, Craig jettisoned our rocket pods and rolled out on a heading toward the PDJ and Long Tieng 30 miles away. Craig executed the emergency procedure checklists while flew to keep the bird in the air.

Craig quickly evaluated the situation and executed the necessary procedures. We had a high cylinder head temperature and no oil pressure. Meanwhile, I made a cool, calm, MAYDAY, MAYDAY, MAYDAY, call on Guard. "Raven 49 heading northwest for a possible bailout over the southern PDJ". I cleared the A-1 lead to join us for a damage check. Craig took control of the stick as I grabbed my camera from my map bag and took a picture of the A-1 evaluating our damage.

A1 Sky Raider, battle damage assessment

Craig slid the canopy aft so he could see better out of the left and right side of the aircraft. Forward visibility was dark oily brown. Craig reminded me to close the canopy before ejection if we had to bail out; which was looking more and more likely. The good news was that the A-1's were on our wing in escort mode so if we bailed out they could facilitate our recovery. An Air America UH1 helicopter was over the southern PDJ ready for a quick pick up if needed. Time warped slowly, and I found myself in the eyes open prayer mode; "Father in Heaven keep us safe, in Jesus' name." Craig, a Christian man, chimed in with, "Buddha, we could use your help too." We shared a short-lived chuckle and sucked deep breaths as we crossed a ridge and vibrated over the southeast PDJ plateau. We are 15 minutes from the Long Tieng valley, but we had to make it over two more ridgelines before we could glide to a landing at LS 20A if the engine quit. We briefly discussed the options; bail out here, or risk a bailout over the sharp karsts mountain features and thick trees en- route to Long Tieng.

"She is holding together ok, Raven 49 is RTB (returning to base) Long Tieng." Craig radioed on guard."

"Good Luck Raven" was the last words we heard from the A-1 lead on our wing.

Craig nursed our bird over the first sharp ridgeline and through the twisting valley walls that towered above us and met the cloud deck at the cliff tops. We were 20 knots above a stall and 400 feet off the ascending valley slopes. There we were, limping home and whispering sweet nothings to that broken and struggling cyclone engine up front. "Come on baby, just a little further." The last ridgeline was above us as Craig attempted to climb just a few more feet. The VVI (vertical velocity indicator) vibrated at around 100 ft per minute. The airspeed was bleeding off to stall, and the eastern end of skyline ridge remained a solid obstacle in our path. The rudder pedals stall warning shook in alarm as Craig nursed down 10 degrees of flaps. The Nomad shuttered and cleared the ridge by almost 10 feet. Down into the valley, we fell in a stall recovery dive as our airspeed increased to final approach speed. "Gear down full stop." We glided to a safe landing covered in sweat and joy. We pulled off the runway and shut down an awesome radial engine.

Moose Carroll, other Ravens and crew chiefs gathered around the valiant AT-28D as the cowl was lifted to reveal a shattered cylinder, push rod, and oil line. The smell of hot Oil smoke perfume drifted over the ramp as we deplaned in sarcastic laughter. I kissed the bird and the ramp and thanked God for all his protection. "Thanks for the PDJ orientation flight Craig, Nice flight" I spoke with relieved sarcasm.

The second set of A-1's was holding below the darkening cloud deck as Craig launched a freshly fueled Bird Dog to continue the air strike against the unlucky 9 level gunner who winged us. I went for a cold beer and some adrenaline withdrawal.

Craig Morrison and the A-1's killed the gun and saved the day for the outpost defenders. This was just another combat mission in the Raven Logbook.

The scenario re-played in my mind several times. Something spiritual had occurred moments after the heavy jolt slammed the right forward cowl and our sputtering motor fought to pull us toward home. I was not in shock as tragedy neared. I was going to fight to survive and overcome. Time compressed, as I had mentally murmured, a just in case, goodbye to my wife and family. I did that often during my Raven tour of duty.

My ejection pins are pulled, the canopy is closed, straps and harness snug tight. Chinstrap cinched, visor down, survival radio on and I think I am ready to rocket on out of here via Yankee extraction.

Craig was smooth on the controls as we descended well below the ridgeline for lack of power. "Well, she almost wants to fly," Craig spoke to himself over the intercom.

"That motor is not going to last very long; she is bleeding hot black oil all over your pretty gray paint quipped the A-1 pilot. "Hey Tiny, take a picture of that Hobo, I want it for my scrapbook," Craig said.

After that narrow escape, I became a different pilot, wiser, blessed to live anew in a gush of gratefulness, grace, and protection. I had been rescued from the myth of self-reliance. Some things are out of our control. We do the best we can and trust our creator for survival. That narrow escape gave me freedom from fear. I would face impending tragedy many times after that incident but having survived once; I always expected the same result. "Fear not." I now believed in miracles! This was emotional sweetness and confidence in a supernatural alliance. In later years, I studied truth and life in the teachings of Christ, Buddha, Confucius, Gandhi, Mandela, and many others teachers. Now I understand the work of salvation, and the forgiveness "for we know not what we do."

That night, Craig and I replayed the day's combat events with laughter, tears of joy and amazing inner energy. We had been fortunate, blessed, and very lucky to escape one more time. We concluded that there must be a reason, a purpose for our survival.

We fought hard and persevered. We recounted the days until we would DROS (Date Return Overseas) to the United States and be reunited with families. I tossed in my sleep like a kickboxer in training for a few hours, and then I slept well and woke early to do it all again, day after day, one mission at a time. In all, I flew over 600 combat missions and logged over 1200 hours of combat time over enemy occupied battlefields. I lost many friends. Freedom is not free!

Chapter 4

https://www.wep11345.com/chapter-4.html

My Ravens

But we in it shall be remembered-
We few, we happy few, we band of brothers;
For he to-day that sheds his blood with me
Shall be my brother; be he ne'er so vile,"
-William Shakespeare, Henry V.

Raven Banditos 1969, G. Greven, H. Allen, T. Carroll, Pop, Dave, J. Bauer, Tom, T. Palmer, W. Platt, T. Harris, W. Kozma, J. Potter, S. Green, Dan.

Henry Lewis Allen, MIA, 26 March 1970, W. Platt collection

Henry Allen, "Hank" Raven 41 was from Florida. He often led us in loud, bawdy song; beer belched, boisterous, off-key song at Long Tieng's Raving Raven Bar. We shared an evening of humor to unwind with excellent pilot friends, techs, specialists, crew chiefs, and radio operators. Who knew they could not sing? Intel's Joe Bauer, AOC leaders Joe Potter, Jerry Rhein, and Tom Palmer bought rounds of libation after losing in darts or shuffleboard at the 404 lounge: no rank separation, no friction, we were a volunteer team generating combat sorties for our General Vang Pao. We celebrated because we still could.

Hank Williams and Johnny Cash lyrics are lost in whiskey slurs. Jerry Greven, Karl Polifka, Mike Byers, Mike Cavanaugh, and Bob Dunbar finished their tour as Ravens and departed the Long Tieng valley. I was the new FAC at LS 20A. Terry "Moose" Carroll, Bill Kozma, and Smoky Green strummed guitars and banjo. Donald "Duck" Craig Morrison, Tom Harris, and Jim "Tea shirt" Strusaker would croon and hoot. 'Stanley" L. Erstad would rhyme in time, as

"Weird" Harold Mesaris would spool a line. Allen Holt, the bellowing Georgia bulldog, could sing well. Craig Duehring became the newbie FAC. Ray de Arrigunaga, Brian "Iron Bomb" Wages, John Fuller, Jeff Thompson, Park Bunker, Chuck Engle, Mark Diebolt, and Bill Lutz joined the fray as battered Ravens rotated to follow-on assignments. Each man picked up the battle tunes in turn and fought with pride.

Project 404 lounge, Greven collection

On special occasions, Donald "Duck" C. Morrison would eat a glass. Someone would bite the head off a snake, drink the blood, and swallow the heart raw in a shot of cheap scotch; in their inebriated imaginations. The Edgar Allen Poe Literary Society (EALPS) vision was alcohol induced, but it was there, and then, that a fellowship of author pilots was conceived with frank sincerity. The rest is history. The senior AOC staff usually parlayed with the elder SKY Spooks, and the weighty planners at the Floyd May-bell SKY bear bar until late at night. Tom and Ray would fly late in the morning when AOC responsibilities allowed. We younger Tigers went to bed earlier to be ready for the pre-dawn launch to find and strike the enemy. We did not discuss the morality of war and the consequences of unexploded ordinance. That conversation would wait until combat missions were well behind us.

We were all General Vang Pao's Hmong fighters; each a relative committed to one another and eventual victory for the Hmong at Long Tieng. VP set the example of ultimate courage. The weight of sacrifices was on his shoulders. He, more than any other knew the price of war. As the responsible leader, he grieved and endured massive pain and loss. VP did not ever submit to defeat. His vision for freedom and equality for his people motivated him through the worst of times. Vang Pao was our Warlord General with a will to succeed. He led from the front lines and took risks along with his soldiers. He was a courageous Leader charged with motivated a shrinking and dispirited army.

Two Ravens were lost on 26 March 1970; "Hank" Allen and Dick Elzinga. They disappeared, and we could not find a trace of their crash site. Then, on 26 April 1970, two more Ravens, Jim Cross, and Dave Reese were shot down and killed by a 37mm anti-aircraft battery just west of the Ban Ban valley. We did our best to find and rescue them; to no avail. We grieved and then got freaky "mad" at the enemy. Vengeance is a powerful drug that warps reality and good judgment. We each asked ourselves, why you brothers and not me? Who will be next?

In D minor, at half cadence, in tearful harmony and pain, we sang a sad song that went something like this…

"Dear Mom, your son is dead,
he bought the farm today,
They shot him down with mighty triple-A.
He made a rocket pass; it was his very last...
They smoked his ass..., with life's last gasp...
He called out for you. "Mom"
Mom, He called out for you."

AT 28D #599, Greven collection

Chapter 5

https://www.wep11345.com/chapter-5.html

Hmong Bravery

The cost of freedom is always high, but Americans have always paid it. And one path we shall never choose, and that is the path of surrender or submission.
-John F. Kennedy

Sentry duty, February 1970, W. Platt collection

The Hmong People have been on the long search for freedom and peace. Many tribal cultures before them stood and fought oppression. Un-unified, outnumbered by better-armed troops and armies, many Meo abandoned their settlements and migrated as remnant tribes to uninhabited mountain ranges across southern China, Laos, Vietnam Thailand, and old Burma. They settled, farmed, and hunted on land not granted to them by governments. Hmong were survivalists, living in the mountains of Phou Bai. They were freedom fighters and masters of Guerilla Warfare. These fighters were two generations beyond flintlocks, crossbows, and spears. The Hmong spirit is a motivation for all tribes, clans, and creeds who would settle for nothing less than equality and the dignity of freedom.

The soldiers were young when they left their villages and were deployed to distant outposts. The women were resilient parents caring for many orphaned children, wounded soldiers, and sisters whose husbands perished in the war. Young girls lovingly carried tiny siblings strapped on their backs as they labored. These amazing women were selfless, graceful, and cheerful in the most austere conditions. They were primitive survivalists carving out hamlets and farms in high valleys. They skillfully lived off the natural resources available in the mountains. Their fruitful gardens produced vegetables, flowers, nuts and the ancient painkilling medicine, black tar opium, and hemp.

Raven John Garrity collection

Raven John Garrity collection

Raven John Garrity collection

Raven John Garrity collection

Raven John Garrity collection

Raven John Garrity collection

Raven John Garrity collection

Raven John Garrity collection

Gossett collection

Gossett collection

Raven John Garrity collection

Friends, Garrity collection

Raven John Garrity collection

W. Platt collection

Refugees, Raven Craig Morrison, 1970, W. Platt collection

Medicines came from plants, roots, and bark. Shaman and midwives
were healers. Good and evil spirits indwelled every mountains rock,
tree, and animal. Ancestors communicate with and bless the living.
Village elders governed hamlet communities by traditions of
equality and communal sharing of resources. I never met a selfish
Hmong. Relatives cared for nurtured the family unit in the scarcity
life's requirements. The Hmong were spiritually connected to the
earth, air, water, fire and the elements of survival. We admired their
peaceful, kind, and sharing nature off the battlefield. We were
welcomed as family and honored with bonds of a soldier's goodwill.

Their Diaspora reminded me of the Israelite tribe's wilderness
journey of Exodus and the brutal displacement of the American
Indian from our western territories. Eventually, more than 200,000
men, women, and children made the journey from refugee camps in
Thailand to America. They earned the opportunity to realize the
freedoms they fought to achieve. Their fight and sacrifice saved
many American lives. Forty thousand Hmong perished fighting

communist oppression in Laos. Tens of thousands were evacuated from their hamlets to overcrowded refugee centers away from the fighting. They suffered but remained cheerful beyond our understanding.

In January 1970, Ravens flew hundreds of escort missions for the armada of helicopters transporting Hmong refugees from villages northwest of LS108 (Mong Souy) to refugee centers much further south. Sam Tong, LS20, Long Tieng, LS 22A, Muong Cha (LS-113), Houei Thong Kho (LS-184) LS 54, and other refugee centers took in, settled, and provided for Hmong families. They escaped the path of a merciless foe ordered to annihilate all resistance and the seed of those who opposed and embarrassed them in battle. Village refugees entered aircraft for the first time in their lives and flew into the unknown. Helicopters and airplanes large and small shuttled them from Lima sites to refugee centers. They said goodbye to a beloved way of life and were taken to an unfamiliar place to survive. They could only take what they could pack and carry on their backs. Hmong women wore their ceremonial clothes and silver adornments in styles and colors that identified their village, clan, and heritage. They reminded me of American immigrants embarking for Ellis Island. Hope remained, but just barely.

We Ravens defended Hmong villages and Lima Sites as if they were our hometowns. Some Ravens became Ameri-Hmong at heart; adopting the spirit of the Chao Pao Khao, "Fly until you die." These Mountains of Phou Bia are more than a symbol of Freedom. They should be the homeland of a very brave, free, independent, and industrious people. Freedom never quits. Old soldiers never give up, and young soldiers never stop bleeding.

General Vang Pao

http://www.t28trojanfoundation.com/vang-pao.html

The Commander stands for the virtues of wisdom, sincerely, benevolence, courage, and strictness. -Sun Tzu

General Vang Pao and his wife,
Hmong New Year, Long Tieng, December 1969,
Greven Collection

Hmong New Year beauty contest, 1969, Greven Collection

General Vang Pao fought with French commandos against the Viet Minh. At age 13, he parachuted with them into the Plaines des Jars to resist the Japanese invasion. He led 850 Hmong through the dense jungles and mountainous terrain of northern Laos attempting to relieve the French at Dien Bien Phu. At that war's end, he joined the Royal Laotian Army (RLA) and eventually was given command of the 10th Infantry Battalion protecting the northern border of Laos. In 1961, he and his Special Guerrilla Units became fierce combat allies of the United States effort to halt the spread of communism in SEA. VP was the only Hmong General. He was the protector of the land and people, an Honorable visionary, a beloved father figure. He was faithful to all that is Hmong; he served Laos and the King. He had a vision of a legitimate, recognized Hmong homeland in Xieng Khouang Province. VP called on his soldiers to sacrifice, and they did. We were all his Hmong fighters, and we liked it. General Vang Pao was a charismatic leader and a master of Guerrilla warfare tactics. Narrow trails over steep, defensible mountain passes connected the hamlets and defensive positions. He knew them all. My Air operation center commanders, Joe Potter and Jerry Rhein, provided General Vang Pao with the best aerial attack aircraft and experienced volunteer aviators available. Aircraft and pilots were VP's artillery and a vital source of real-time battlefield intelligence. He led from the front, and he was often present at, or above, the battle in progress.

LS 20A, O1, "SPIN" approach, W. Platt collection

Special Guerilla Units

Standing on the defensive indicates insufficient strength; attacking, a superabundance of strength. -Sun Tzu

Thai outpost, PDJ, W. Platt collection

MRll Special Guerilla Units (SGUs) were mostly Hmong battalions made up of three rifle companies and a headquarters unit. They were a mobile strike force led by Hmong leaders and advised by American army attaché personnel and CIA field officers. General Vang Pao controlled mission deployments and led major offensive and defensive actions. Armed with rifles, grenades, mortars, bazookas and recoilless rifles, they re-positioned from hilltop to hilltop by Air America helicopters. All logistic support of these troops was made by helicopter or fixed wing low altitude airdrop. Road watch teams and patrols from the hilltops positions were serviced by air. Challenging weather and local snipers often delayed resupply. Circumstances alter plans, and we mastered the improvisation mode of operations.

SGU, PDJ, 1969, Garrity collection

General Vang Pao launched a major offensive against the NVA/Pathet Lao forces in the fall of 1969. American airpower sustained the offensive against enemy positions on the PDJ. Operation About Face was a huge success. The Hmong reclaimed the PDJ for the first time since 1960. They captured 25 Soviet PT-76 tanks, 640 heavy weapons, 2,500 tons of ammunition, and 1,700 tons of food. Hmong units lost hundreds of soldiers. There were no more Hmong replacements, so the Lao army sent SGU's from MRlll and MRlV to assist. Those SGU's were another ethnic minority called the Lao Theung. They also were advised by round-eyed Americans. Additional Thai units and pilots entered secret war arena. By the end of the fighting more than 4500, Thai soldiers were killed, and many more were wounded. US bombing increased in response to enhanced PAVN infiltration onto the PDJ. For the Hmong at the outposts, there was no relief and no evacuations. Fight until you die, and many did.

A lasting victory was unsustainable due to insufficient numbers of fighters. In January 1970, the NVA mustered two divisions of their regular army to methodically recapture the lost PDJ and threaten the major Hmong bases at Long Tieng and Sam Tong. For the first time, Ambassador Godley was authorized to employ B-52s to halt the PAVN offensive on the southern PDJ as the strength of the Hmong waned.

The Hmong people I knew were proud, independent, hospitable, curious, shy, industrious survivalists. Their drive, energy, and unfailing optimism in the face of terror trained us in courage and fortitude. With Hmong families soon under attack within the Long Tieng valley, everyone did their duty with selfless purpose.

SGU outpost, PDJ, Greven collection

SGU Outpost PDJ , 1969, Garrity collection

Tan Pop Buell, Gossett collection

"Robin" Scout Translators:

Robin Moua Ly, Chief Robin Yang Bee, Robin Yia Kha Cha Pao Khao, W. Platt collection

Thai mechanic "Boo"   Robin scout Moua Ly,   W. Platt collection

Robin scout Wa Ger Cheng (Scar)

Francis Vang, Robin scout, Chao Pha Khao pilot

A natural linguist, Francis Vang was a student in Vientiane when he was drafted into military service. He was an excellent scout and survived several crashes and bailouts with Ravens before he entered Cha Pao Khao pilot training in Thailand.

General Vang Pao's airborne scouts adopted the radio call sign "Robin." These men were often veteran Special Guerilla Unit (SGU) soldiers with a thorough knowledge of the Hmong Landing Site defenses, tactics, and unit locations. They were VP's eyes and ears above the battle area. They would relay VP's specific instructions to SGU commanders. Robins were given the authority to validate targets for air strikes. They represented VP. Together we shared the responsibility not to drop bombs on civilians or the friendlies.

The O-1 Birddog was our light, tandem two-seat, 213hp single engine, observation and strike control aircraft made by Cessna. We carried a Forward Air Guide, call sign Robin, who translated for us and coordinated with our special guerrilla unit ground forces. As a group, the Robins were courageous and well skilled at finding targets. This was their homeland, and they knew the territory by landmarks and canyon walls. They were skilled and motivated in finding the way home to Long Tieng when smoky haze, fog, or storm restricted visibility to a few miles. They studied us and reported our skills, aggressiveness, and judgment directly to General Vang Pao.

One Robin died in a Raven backseat, shot by enemy gunners. Many Hmong Robins were wounded while flying with Ravens. One flew the aircraft home and landed when the Raven was severely wounded. These men like Yia Kha, Francis Vang, Yang Bee, Moua Ly, Wa Ger Cheng (Scar), Yia Kha, and Moonface were men I flew with often. Working closely with these young Hmong men was an honor and an exercise in mutual trust. They were motivated warriors fighting for the safety of their families, clan, leaders, and country. Wa Ger Cheng died in Laos when the Vietnamese attacked his village, and he flew to the rescue of his Uncle fighting there. Some encouraged us to fly and fight Low and Slow for the best visual acuity. Yia Kha, Moua Ly, and Fong Vang were selected to train and fly the T28 fighter aircraft of the RLAF in 1971. Now, pilots, they joined the ranks of other Hmong Cha Pao Khao heroes. We respected them and took their advice. We learned the Hmong tactics that made us a powerful synergistic force against a much larger enemy unit. Other brave Robins were Wa Lee Moua who died when F4 pilot dropped CBU by mistake in Long Tieng. Tou Houa Xiong was shot down with Raven 23 on the PDJ. His remains have never been recovered. An enemy rocket in Long Tieng killed Bee Vang. Kia Tou Thao, Yee Yang, and Ly Seng were outstanding fighters and interpreters. Teng Ly was shot and killed by the enemy while in the back seat of a Raven aircraft. They were an amazing group of young men who served their people and freedom cause with distinction. For me, they epitomized the best of Hmong virtues.

Robins were a comfort in many ways. If forced to walk, rather than fly home, they could lead us back, through enemy controlled territory to friendly settlements or outposts. On the other hand, Robins were an added responsibility. Their lives depended on our sound flight skills and wise risk assessments.
I would take more risks and flew with more aggression when alone. Concern for my passenger's safety was a priority responsibility. The additional 150 lbs of man and equipment compromised the O1's already underpowered performance.
Robin scout translators worked with Raven Forward Air Controllers in O1, T-28, and U-17 aircraft. They spoke many Lao minority dialects, Hmong, Thai, and English to convey the needs of the ground commanders to the Forward air controller who in turn would brief and direct the US fighter pilots for weapons delivery. They had the eyes of eagles and knew the NVA routines, ploys, and traditional hiding places. We trusted each other with our lives and quickly became partners and brothers in arms.
They endured our gyrating combat maneuvers all day long. On the way back to Long Tieng, we encouraged them to fly the aircraft. The scenario of a wounded, unconscious Raven being flown home safely encouraged us to give them flying time on return flights to L20A.

The Robins would fly every day. Often they would team up with one Raven for consecutive missions. Most seemed to enjoy the happy mystery of flight and became accustomed to the jinking and jiving ride of combat.

Upon the mountaintop redoubts and down on the Laotian Plain of Jars Special Guerrilla Units (SGU's) of General Vang Pao's Hmong Army fought off the advancing NVA with light arms, mortars, and recoilless rifles. The NVA had large mortars, cannons, and rockets that could bombard the primitive trench and bunker outposts of the Hmong Fighters from a concealed, out of range, distance.

The Forward Air Guides (FAGs) on the ground with the SGU battalions could often locate or relay the positions of the enemy. They had individual call signs like Rainbow, Swamp Rat, Black Lion, or Showboat. Often there was an American CAS advisor there, but most of the communication on the VHF radio was between the FAG (Forward Air guides) and the Robin scout translators. The CAS officers encouraged, trained, and advised this vital radio operator cadre.

The Robin knew the lay of the land, where the friendly patrols were, and the enemy locations. They knew where they wanted the ordinance to impact and the type of anti-aircraft fire anticipated. Then the Robin had to communicate that information to the Raven Pilot, confirm the understanding between them using a pointed finger over the shoulder and Hmong-English-French, thumbs up.

Then the Raven would figure the exact coordinates from his map and communicate the critical information to the Fighters and ABCCC ensuring that they knew exactly where the friendly troops were positioned. The Raven would fire a white-prosperous rocket to mark the first target, clear the fighters Hot, meaning cleared to release their ordinance on the target. The Air Guides would continue to request tactical air support on specific locations until the heavy ordinance was expended on the targets. The Raven and Robin would then glass, (use binoculars) in the strike zone and descend to provide a Bomb damage assessment as the smoke cleared. The Fighter-bombers would save some of their 20mm in case the Raven experienced ground fire. Often the SGU would send out a team to complete a more extensive BDA. The teamwork of the Hmong Forward Air Guides, Robins and Raven pilots enabled the outnumbered and outgunned SGU's to eliminate threats that were out of their weapons range or hidden close to the SGU perimeter.

Bomb Damage Assessment is a vague term. We were trained to take a good look, to estimate the damage, enumerate the destruction, and estimate the casualties. Let me describe this correctly. Three fighters just dropped six tons of high explosive blast and pain on some NVA soldier's outpost. Now he is coming up out of his deep spider hole to see who is still alive. He is mad, his ears are ringing, and his friends are wounded. Now, overhead is that little airplane that attacked his world. If he can shoot, he did shoot everything he could shoot, at you."

BDA trucks, Rt. 6, Greven collection

Raven FACs low level, post-strike, bomb damage assessment was risky business. Secondary explosions and the angry ground fire were always expected. We reported petroleum fires, busted bunkers, trenches, caves, creek bed hideouts, guns, trucks, troops, and tanks destroyed.

Treetop BDA was dangerous for the mind and body. We brought destruction, day after day, a small patch of earth at a time. We are numbed and shocked to accept someone's tragedy as normal. Sympathy and compassion were-post flight afterthoughts. In the war zone, we fight by day, drink to sleep and forget what we did to other men.

Many of us would say, "If we have to fight, end it quickly and decisively with shock in the downtown party headquarters. Turn off their power, burst the dams, and keep our aquatic mines in their harbor. Pour on the heat with minimal loss of allies' lives. Keep up the pressure until they break and fully understand the consequences of their decisions."

The bean counters at headquarters need to enumerate air strike results to justify their effective use of expensive air power assets. The pressure for tangible BDA results and body counts in Vietnam got so bad that some FACs reported what the Generals wanted to hear. Yes Sir, big BDA with many KIAs.

American boys grew up being the Lone Ranger with silver bullets, protecting their neighbor by shooting bad guys. Hmong boys grew up losing family members and experiencing the grief of war. We often counted the days remaining until we would go home. The Hmong were home, and they would fight to the terrible end. What we shared in common was fragile life and optimism for a better tomorrow. We were a team against the opposition who planned our defeat at their cost of a million men. While at war, I made no time to weigh and contemplate the immorality of unexploded bombs, herbicides, and napalm burns. So that American families should never experience desperate war on our soil, we responded to a battlefield in the Hmong front yard. Our intentions were honorable while our methods were costly in allied suffering. The post-war clean up will last a century.

Chao Pha Khao Pilots, December 1970

http://www.t28trojanfoundation.com/chao-pha-khao.html

The good fighter will be terrible in his onset, and prompt in his decision.
-Sun Tzu

Chao Pha Khao Flight Lead Yang Xiong

Chao Pha Khao Vang Cheng   Chao Pha Khao Vang Sue

Chao Pha Khao Vang Cheng

Maj. Yang Xiong was the Cha Pao Khao flight leader; Lt. Vang Cheng and Capt. Vang Sue were his trusty wingman. These pilots flew combat together every day. They fought as brothers against AA gunners and bunkered PAVN troops. Low level, random heading, impromptu strike tactics were their specialty. They dueled with guns for a living. They defeated 37mm AAA, many days each week. Their flight was constantly maneuvering, and attacking from every altitude and direction. Like wasps covering each other's run into the target, delivery, and escape. The Hmong pilots were precision air to mud strikers, accurate, intuitive teamwork at its best. They were the most aggressive, low and slow fighter pilots I worked with in SEA. Their attack was like an un-choreographed dance. They flew situational maneuvers to avoid the enemy gunners lead. Impulse headings and improvised altitudes put bombs, rockets, CBU, napalm, and twin 50's on the target. Occasionally, incognito, AOC air commando Jerry Rhein joined their attack formation as an "advisor."

25 December 1969

We had been controlling airstrikes east of the PDJ. As we searched for targets my Hmong master scout, interpreter, tour guide, and friend, Wa Jer Cheng (Scar), tapped me on the left shoulder. He pointed to 10 o'clock low for 6 miles. "Chao Pha Khao" was all he said.

I had heard amazing reports of their exceptional skills from other Ravens. I grinned, and thought to myself; I have seen the rest, are these pilots the best?

Four, fully armed T-28'were circling a thinly wooded tree line between a creek and rice patties. Scar monitored their radio frequency while I maneuvered outside and above their formation's bubble. Scar glassed the target area while I put the sun at our back. We were now well positioned to monitor this air to mud bombardment.

Flight leader, Yang Xiong, dove to treetop level to conceal his long, low approach toward structures, bunkers, and tanks. Realizing that an attack was imminent two 12.7 gun crews cast back their camouflage nets to shoot at the three stalking fighters 2,000 ft. above. The guns were separated by a hundred yards and had three man gun crews inside deep pits. Looking through my field glasses, I could see the camouflaged nets open, and two 12.7 machineguns appeared. These anti-aircraft guns had three man crews.

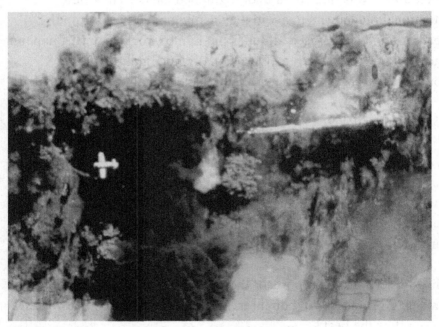

Chao Pha Khao AT28 airstrike, W. Platt collection

The wavering, growls from the T28s orbiting overhead drew the gunners attention and masked the screaming roar of Maj. Xiong's approach. He was undetected as he released a napalm canister. The enemy guns were pointed in the wrong direction as he flashed by. The napalm slammed into the trees and was ignited by a stream of white phosphorous. The fireball engulfed the first gun position as the petroleum fire's black smoke plume temporarily blinded the second gun crew's view. The guns took a lead on the Maj. Xiong's T-28 departure, CPK 2, Capt. Vang Sue was already diving in on the second gun position. The three-man gun crew disappeared in a flash. Lt. Vang Cheng rolled in on shallow bunkers and skipped a canister of napalm through the trees on two camouflaged PT76 tanks in a courtyard. Chao Pao Khao #4 was Jerry Rhein, our Air Operation Center commander. The flight circled overhead in loose trail until one of the pilots spotted a target and rolled in for the kill. The scattered ground fire erupted in orange, yellow flashes that were quickly extinguished by more bombs and napalm. Like a choreographed whirling dance, the T-28's swarmed on the NVA soldiers and guns below.

T 28 strike, Greven collection

The CPK continued to circle allowing the smoke to clear. Soon they were making gun passes on the remaining structures and burning trucks. Maj. Xiong pulled up hard left to re-join the CPK formation. On the ground, ammunition was cooking off, and black billowing smoke rose from several petroleum tank fires. The first fuel tank was now in flames. Vang Cheng, CPK 2, had rolled in with a Stuka steep dive on guns and delivered a slick, 250 lb bomb into the remaining pit. In sequential 4-part harmony, Vang Sue, strung duel lines of cluster bomb units (CBU) over this fiery hell. CPK 4 was next. He came off the perch and zeroed in on covered storage bunkers. He released a single 250 lb bomb that blew the log roof completely off the hide. The wheel formation tightened as CPK pilots acquired new targets and plunged at the bunkers along the creek bank. Orange small arms, muzzle-flashes ceased in fire and explosion. Each tango maneuvered behind his predecessor to suppress the ground fire. Their timing and coordination were superb. Their radio chatter was constant as they discussed the target threats and locations. Each Tango carried a mix of ordinance that reflected the pilots preferred weapons of choice. Napalm and Cluster Bomb Units (CBU), were effective using low, flat delivery while bombs and HE rockets facilitated a higher release altitude and called for a steep delivery. Repeatedly, this gaggle of tenacious Tangos pounded the PAVN positions. After a final gun pass, we saw four victory rolls and a formation rejoin. CPK flight was RTB (Return to Base) L20A. No Joke! That is what Happened!

T 28D, Greven collection

Scar and I cheered in appreciation of these CPK pilots' incredible tactics, teamwork, and accuracy. It takes a lot to impress me; I worked some fantastic fighter pilots. Yes, that was the most effective airstrike this FAC witnessed during my year of the war. I would direct hundreds of more air strikes, but this was the one I remember most of all.

These CPK flew into the valley of the shadow of death, to do their duty; to defend friends, and family, in the hope of freedom. Those three warriors, like Lee Leu before them, dove their winged chariots into battle and emerged closer to freedom. They won this battle. The next was just a few hours away. Their motto was "Fly until you die."

I wanted to meet these men, shake their hands, and share a moment before it was too late.

The CPK had no restrictions or limitations, no rules of engagement. When General Vang Pao said to strike a target, they did. The flight leader knew the capabilities of his wingmen. These pilots flew and fought together seven days a week. They could find, evaluate, and strike a target immediately. They received their strike authority directly from VP. They could speak directly with their ground commanders and receive real-time intelligence on enemy locations and movements. CPK pilots were all shooters. They each would fly six to eight hours every day defending Special Guerilla Unit operations. They were airborne hunters with instincts for attack and bravery in battle. Strong leadership, cumulative combat experience, personal pride in excellence, brotherly love, and enduring teamwork enabled them to excel in the pinpoint air to mud applications of airpower. Close family and cultural relationships fused them into a united force of very skilled, combat pilots. They had a plan ready to deal with each variation of a target, terrain, and weather. Their improvised use of low-level tactics enabled them to locate, strike, and destroy normally inaccessible targets. They flew on the edge of performance and adapted quickly to overcome threats. They were motivated by love for their people and a General who respected their skill and sacrifice. These mountains and valleys were their home. They were protecting their families from another barbaric enemy that wanted to eliminate them all. They would fight for freedom, autonomy, and ownership of their lands. That was not to be. They endeavored to persevere as allies abandoned them to persecution. They suffered desperation, the diaspora of another long migration, war refugee immigration, and long family separations. All they wanted was to live free on their land.

Lee Lue was known as the very best Hmong pilot of the war. He perished in combat from a direct hit from 37mm anti-aircraft artillery round 4 months before I arrived at Long Tieng. Flight leader Maj. Yang Xiong and his loyal wingman Vang Sue and Vang Cheng were my contemporaries. They were "Low and Slow," fighter pilots at one with their mountains; flying among the spirits of their ancestors, protecting hilltop redoubts harboring Special Guerilla Units (SGU's). For me, they characterized the Hmong fighting spirit. We breathed the same cool air and flew toward the same hopeful horizon of together. Their courage and skill will not be forgotten.

These T28 pilots were every bit as accurate as USAF A1 fighter-bombers. They carried a third of the weapons load and stayed on station a third of the time, but their fight was close to home, so missions were short.

Back on the flight line at LS 20A, I approached this trio of Hmong Chao Pha Khao pilots with a big grin and a handshake as they headed for lunch in their jeep. They spoke aviation English and greeted me with the acceptance and hospitality of brothers in arms.

Of 37 original Hmong pilots who took the silent pledge to "fly until death," 20 survived the Secret Laotian Civil War.

North American AT-28D, W. Platt collection

Thai, Raven, Air America, and Water pump volunteers.

O1, T28, O1. PDJ, W. Platt collection

Dawn patrol, Greven collection

Chapter 6

https://www.wep11345.com/chapter-6.html

The O-1 Bird Dog and U-17B

We remember and re-live the sounds of battle, the punctuation of the round as it pierced our aluminum chariot, the adrenaline-pumping sense of the gunfire below. Heard on radios, our controlled voices mask the surges of our energy, as we dared to live. We hear the desperate sound of the emergency beeper as it signaled that one of us has fallen. We feel the silent thunder of our pounding hearts. Yes, we remember!

Raven O1 Bird Dog, W. Platt Collection

The Cessna O-1 Bird Dog was the standard Raven FAC aircraft. She was chosen for her simplicity of operation and maintainability in austere locations. She was stable and forgiving in flight. A tail-dragger, she was famous for ground looping pilots timid with ruder. Her power was 213 horses giving her a cruising speed of 100 mph (85 knots). With two, 20-gallon fuel tanks in the wings, the O1 could operate up to four hours and 15 minutes per sortie. She had two seats in tandem, one for the pilot and a second rear seat for a Robin, scout passenger. The O1 was not a short takeoff and landing (STOL) aircraft, but even in the mountains, a 900 ft runway was acceptable. The Bird Dog had less range than the U-17 or T-28. The Oscar had no armor and was slow to climb, (500 feet per minute, maybe), wings level at lift-over-drag max. The plane was susceptible to ground fire during the slow climbing exit from a target. Her fuel tanks were not self-sealing which made her vulnerable to wing fires. However, she had the best visibility of all the aircraft Ravens used for our FAC mission. An additional feature was the clear plexus-glass panels over the pilots head, allowing us to track fighter aircraft above us easily. Instrumentation was basic, and the O-1 had marginal night flying capability. All O-1 Bird Dogs used by the Ravens were painted light gray, with a red stripe across the top of the wing. Aircraft identification numbers were stenciled on the tail. There was no U.S. or other national markings on the aircraft. The O-1, like other FAC aircraft, carried the AN/ARC-44 FM radio, the AN/ARC-73 VHF radio, and the AN/ARC-45 UHF radio (later replaced by the ARC-51BX).

Raven O1, alone and behind enemy lines, Greven collection

I flew the O-1 with active rudder and quick trim wheel adjustments. We often flew her out of trim intentionally. We set up an oscillating slight climb or dive. As the airspeed bleeds off in the ascent, the lift decreases yielding a pitch reversal to a slight dive. As the airspeed increases in the dive, the lift increases and the nose rises producing another slight climb. The cycle repeats. Add some rudder to the equation and the O1 is an elusive, difficult bird to hit with small arms.

This technique leaves both hands free for radios, maps, binoculars, camera, grenade launcher, and cockpit switches. Our eyes were rarely focused inside the cockpit, and then only for a glance at the gages. The sound of the changing RPM clewed the pilot to needed airspeeds adjustments as he searched the ground below. The flight path was a continuing maneuver to optimize our vision down and out the open side windows. When low and slow our flight path needed to be as elusive and unpredictable as possible. We jinked. That technique worked for a lot of us.

The Cessna U-17B

The U-17B was the military version of the civilian Cessna 185 Sky wagon. She could carry four passengers if needed and a bunch of ammo or beer. A variable pitch prop attached to a 300 hp Continental engine provided higher speed when needed. She had a good climb rate and long 7-hour legs. Her stall speed was 15 knots higher than the O1, but her brakes were very effective with the flaps retracted on touchdown. Short field landing distances 'were a bit longer than the O1. Full flap slips brought us down in a hurry. She could power through a stall recovery with minimal loss of altitude. Lightweight, her flaws included the side-by-side seating that made visibility out of the right side window challenging. She did not have ceiling windows like the O1, so the acquisition of fighters at altitude sometimes required wild gyrations in the horizontal plane. She had a yoke with a heavier feel, and her roll rate was too slow even with a rudder kick. I loved her anyway and found her to be a survivable FAC platform with reasonable speed, load and climb capability. She was night capable with a Tacan, DME, and adequate panel lighting. After a month flying the O1 in MRll, I was given a U 17, operators' manual and told to "GO FLY." No check out, just "GO Fly"; I did. The next day, I was the U-17 Instructor pilot checking out other Ravens in the "wagon" She was a fine bird but a larger target!

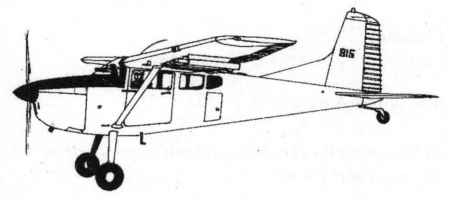

U17B

Chapter 7

https://www.wep11345.com/chapter-7-.html

The North American AT-28D-5

Who maketh the clouds his chariot: who walketh upon the wings of the wind?

T28, LS 20A, W. Platt Collection

I loved flying the AT28D-5. In the beginning, she surprised me with antics. The T-28 would roll as soon as your hand came off the stick. She required constant attention and loving corrections of trim. The low wing of the T-28 made target acquisition and monitoring out the side canopy a challenge. We slid opened the canopy for visual reconnaissance and closed it to control a fighter strike; she was hot, and her cyclone motor was the rumbling sound of freedom. Monitoring ground action required a minimum of 45 degrees of bank, plus a few g's, to fix focus on a specific area for more than a few seconds. I flew to inverted and back again often to track target activity and ordinance impact. Looking down at a target through the top of the Tango canopy was the best seat in the house. Looking forward through the three bladed prop, gun-site, and thick curved canopy was a visual compromise. A few times I had to fire the 2.75 white-prosperous marking rockets while inverted to ensure accuracy. The Tango speed-brake made her a stable Stuka like dive-bomber. FAC mission dive angles were low and shallow and close in. The acceleration, dive, strike, climb, and zoom escape ability of the North American T 28D was a lifesaver many times. She was a tough bird with a monster 1400+ hp engine, two-stage blower safety-wired to the first stage, and a triple-bladed prop up front. She just kept running on 8 of 9 jugs after serious battle damage.

In early March 1970, I began flying the North American AT-28D. I loved her performance and weapons load of 28 rockets and guns. For a short time, free-fire zones were established in the Ban Ban Valley. Armed reconnaissance was the most exciting mission we flew as FACs.

"Yes, I named her "Tanga Nomad," she said I flew her best. I wanted to believe her, so did all the rest."

Jerry Rhein, my boss, and one of the greatest fighter pilots ever gave me a T-28 flight manual and checklist. Learn these by Wednesday, he said. You have earned the right to fight with better equipment. I thanked him with a grin. I checked out in the T-28D5 at Udorn, RAFB Thailand. My instructor was a special operator who had been training allied pilots to fly this trainer fighter. I remember thinking that his job was probably more dangerous than mine was. Maybe the military assistance program and special operations were in my future. I liked the idea. Seven patterns and landings, and 3 GCA's under the hood later, I was ready for a high key, power off, full flap approach to a full stop landing. We turned off at the 1500-foot taxiway with ease. The crosswind component was twenty knots. "Piece of cake." The next day we went to the target range for guns and rocket training. I liked it. After a heavy emergency procedure and flight manual oral grilling, my instructor signed my T-28D5 qualification.

I flew back to the Laotian frontier in my aging attack fighter singing songs along the way. I did some max performance maneuvers of my design, willerdillia maxim us. In the air, over Phou Bia Mountain, I named my powerfully sweet chariot "Tanga Nomad." From then on, I spoke to her as a new adoring lover. She could purr or roar and I stroked her throttle as she did. I recognized her high angle of attack stall vibration warning and respected her quick pivot reversals. With opposite rudder lead-in, her snap roll rate was exceptional. At full power, close to the ground, nearing the stall, flaps ten, she would turn like a purple martin and power to the climb without a whimper or shudder. Wow, what a leap in ability this aluminum lovely gave me. Her feel, and response were tight and nimble. She had duel 50 cal machine guns in her shoulders, and six hardpoints below her wings securing four 2.75 in rocket pods. Each pod held seven rockets. Tanga's endurance was about three hours providing me with plenty of time to finish the fight. She usually carried 28 rockets, a mix of white phosphorous, high explosive and flechettes. Tanga was an accurate strafe and rocket delivery platform. Her climb rate, armament, and Yankee Extraction Seat compensated for her restricted visibility and occasional stubborn attitude.

"Naughty Tanga Nomad"
By: William E. Platt

I named her "Tanga Nomad," she said I flew her best,
I wanted to believe her, so she flew me to her nest...

I fell in Love with her radial jugs; nine, and hot for hugs,
Her empennage so sturdy, her rudder spanking bugs,
Twin fifties graced her shoulders, six hardpoints above her knees,
I love a girl who dresses tough and wants to please not tease.
Her mysteries, mine for asking; her contours, a joy to see,
She wanted a daring pilot, now; She knew that he was me.
Again, daring pilot, come and fly, be free.
In the sky together, you and me are we.

Yes, I named her "Tanga Nomad"; she said I was her best.
I needed to believe her, and so did all the rest...

T28D Long Tieng 1970, W. Platt Collection

Chapter 8

https://www.wep11345.com/chapter-8.html

The Hump

Yea, though I fly through the valley of the shadow of death, I will fear no evil: Psalms 23:4

Hump Valley gauntlet to the PDJ, W. Platt Collection

Every pilot who flew from LS20A to the PDJ and back again, remembers "The Hump." This is where the mountains meet the low clouds, and the gantlets of guns begin. The choice was to fly above the clouds and search for a gap in the clouds to spiral down through in the target area or fly below the clouds and search for a hole to escape up and out. I hoped to "See and Avoid" other aircraft and the hidden hostile guns in the gap ahead. The choice to enter a sucker whole and explore below low clouds was dangerous and necessary when the Special Guerrilla Units (SGU's) needed immediate assistance.

We flew by sight, intuition, instinct, visual acuity, judgment, and prayer. Adjust the altitude, attitude, and speed above the stall for the situation at hand. We learned survival tricks of the trade from observing and mimicking the tried and proven ways of the Air America and CAS Pilots. We compared notes and listened intently to the trial and error accounts of other Ravens. We adapted as the situation constantly changed. The Golden Rule, in the Golden Triangle, was to maintain aircraft control; analyze the situation; and, take the appropriate action. Spur of the moment decisions based on seasoned experience and the current circumstances was the sign of a master FAC. We controlled up to thirty fighter sorties a day during good weather.

Rain, fog, and poor visibility worked to the NVA's advantage. They traveled in the open when we were weathered out. On clear days, they went deep undercover at the first sound of aircraft.

On a calm, overcast day, enemy soldiers would hear a low, slow aircraft 5 miles away. They had several minutes to hunker down, cover up or take aim. They knew the O-1 was a scout looking for trouble. Disciplined and patient, they only fired their weapons under officer orders. The shooting began when they sensed discovery or chose to draw attention away from another location of import. The bigger the gun, the more precious the resource they protect.

The Ambassador's Rules Of Engagement (ROE") were written to protect commanders, our pilots, civilians, and friendly forces. For the most part, the ROE's were common sense. We obeyed the Ambassadors Rules of Engagement. They were consistent with my values and personal combat ethics.

ROE clearance delays did result in some missed targets of opportunity. I am thankful that I did not cause any friendly-fire incidents or have to hump the guilt of ending innocents.

Mobile targets vanished under the canopy in minutes. The time to coordinate approval, rendezvous, bomber-brief and employment often required thirty minutes or longer. Our need was for quick strike capability. Enemy supplies were said to be in abandoned settlement structures. I found enemy outposts and bunkers camouflaged among the ancient Jars of the PDJ. We resented the restrictions that compromised or delayed our ability to strike valid targets immediately when found. I was grateful that no one ordered me to strike enemy civilian settlements.

The U.S. ROE's did not apply to Lao, Thai, or Hmong bomber pilots. They hit everything their commanders deemed non-friendly or of enemy value. The Lao/Hmong military commanders made the strike decisions and approved the targets in MR ll while I was there. The customer advised and provided the logistics and hardware to enable offensive and defensive operations. We all improvised and solved the combat challenges of the moment as effectively as possible.

Ambassador Godley coordinated preplanned targeting lists. I understood that the Lao Prime Minister approved each area bombed. The target approval process was cumbersome, slow, but effective given the goal to minimize collateral damage and fratricide incidents. We were fighting to win while the Ambassador's plan was to delay and prepare allied Lao forces for the inevitable US skedaddle. With Hmong units depleted, the rush to train and equip southern Lao SGU units to defend the Royal government surged.

In January, February, and March 1970 there was a lot of combat on the PDJ. The NVA counter attack was multiple blitzkrieg waves of ground assault men and equipment. Small PAVN units dispersed across the entire PDJ along every road and stream. Emergency calls for a FAC were constant. Troops-in-contact battles were frequent. Lives and tactical positions were lost or reclaimed each day.

"The ROE for SAR: A Jolly Green aircraft and crew were occasionally positioned at Long Tieng. Usually, they were on alert at Udorn two hours south of LS 20A. They could not go on a rescue mission without A-1 cover and support. The A1's were on alert at Udorn, an hour away. Air America helicopters could, and did, reacted immediately to Search and Rescue events. These cool operators often picked up our downed crewmembers before enemy forces or Jolly Greens could respond. They were selflessly and ignored the danger. They just flew in unarmed to make the pickup.

We lost four Raven pilots MIA/KIA in the spring of 1970. Many more aircraft were hit by ground fire and nursed home. Two Ravens were recovered on the PDJ by Air America. The Jollies rescued several Fighter-bomber crews shot down over the HCMT.

"The senior Ravens and AOC met each morning and evening with General Vang Pao, the CIA customer, Jerry Daniels, and his staff to coordinate military plans and operations for that day.

Jerry Rhein was the MRll Air Operations Center commander in January 1970. He earned exceptional confidence and respect from General Vang Pao who recognized a no non-sense warrior with skills. Personally, I believed we were bombing the wrong country. Our ordinance belonged in downtown Hanoi, not rural Laos. The "Big Picture" was unclear, and well my beyond understanding. We played the hand we were dealt with the best of our ability. It was the dry season, early 1970, and the PAVN troops and heavy equipment advanced across the PDJ as our Lao/ Hmong, and Thai allies withdrew from forward positions to regroup for the defense of around Long Tieng.

The Threat

The major threat to Ravens flying in Laos below 1500' was from small arms ground fire and mobile ZPU"s. Heavy machine guns were slow to aim, elevate, and track aircraft. Maneuvering FACs and fighters were a difficult target when not flying predictable patterns. Unfortunately, our USAF formal training instilled repetitious box-patterns. Our predictable inbound headings and altitude enabled experienced gunners to anticipate fighter positions and their intercept lead points.

Our jet fighter pilots trained to follow the leader around "the box" retracing ground tracks and altitudes in a predictable sequence. One after another, over the same turn points, with the same dive angles, airspeeds, and weapons release points. With each pass, the guns became more accurate as gunners made refined corrections. Fast-movers flying common patterns were most vulnerable as they dived at 30 or 45 degrees at the target, and, as they pulled up and away after ordinance release. For that reason, I recommended that they release all ordinance on the first pass. A1's and T-28's usually varied their run in headings after surveying the target on the first pass. Highly experienced flight leaders with hard-crew wingman could coordinate random headings without running into each other or the FAC.

Experienced A1 and T-28 pilots attacked anti-aircraft weapons with random headings, altitudes, and dive angle. They used a variety of ordinance to confuse the NVA gunner's alignment and timing. Bombardment smoke, concussion, destruction, and chaos in the target area forced gunners underground. When the smoke cleared, we flew low to assess the bomb damage.

The NVA mounted ZPU-2, 14.5mm, dual barrel AA guns on a 360-degree swivel turret. This crew serviced, anti-aircraft weapons on mobile four-wheel drive BTR40A armed personnel carriers recon-vehicles were deadly accurate. They were radio equipped and often defended headquarter locations. These mobile guns were our greatest threat. They were rapid-fire, with the ability to quickly traverse their weapon azimuth and declination. With near vertical elevation, they could line you up and shoot you down from an effective range of almost a mile. Jinking, swooping, swerving, non-repetitious orbit tracks, ranges, and altitudes proved to be my best defense.

Twenty-three and thirty-seven mm AAA were usually stationary weapons in pits or rings with a 360-degree field of fire. They often protected high-value targets within a few hundred meters of their location. Their effective range was well over a mile with adjustable airburst altitudes. Tracers and airburst sightings were rare but memorable.

The most used heavy AAA weapon fired against Ravens was the 37mm, ranging out to a mile and one-half. The 37mm guns had a five round magazine, with a sixth round in the chamber. Their rhythm was distinct and memorable.

Chapter 9

https://www.wep11345.com/chapter-9.html

Choke Point Phou Nok Kok

"Kill ten of our soldiers for every one of yours, with those odds, you lose, and we win."   ***Ho Chi Minh***

Phon Nok Kok SGU supplies, W. Platt collection

Black Lion" (BL) was the radio call sign for General Vang Pao's most eastern mountaintop outpost, Phon Nok Kok. A Hmong SGU Battalion advised by Jim Atkins, and his SGU Battalion from MR IV advised by Will Green was dug in and threatened Route 7 traffic. The 312th NVA Division had been reconstituted and were ready to advance west to re-occupy the PDJ.

Our BL mountaintop perch in the dirt overlooked a narrow throat where Rt.7 twisted through mountain gaps to connect North Vietnam, and Ban Ban valley with the Laotian Plain of Jars. This was a classic choke point where a few hundred brave men with small arms, a recoilless rifle, claymore mines, and grenades, a French 75 canon, and air power artillery could momentarily stymie a juggernaut Army's advance.

Will Green and Jim Atkins were the Classified American Source (CAS), "field officers," advising the entrenched warriors on PNK. Their presence was a major force multiplier; America's skin in the game in MRll.

The People's Army of Vietnam (PAVN) soldiers needed a motivational victory after the humiliating retreat and defeat by VP's "About Face" campaign of 1969. Envision the helicopter assault on strategic PDJ hilltops while Royal Laotian paratroopers, assaulted from RLAF C-47 aircraft. Indigenous, Hmong guerilla paratroopers fought to re-occupy Xieng Khouang City and her long airfield dubbed Lima Lima. This was an inexcusable defeat that infuriated General Vo Nguyen Giap. He doubled down and ordered two full divisions to re-take and hold the Xieng Khouang Province. To counter this escalation, the US Ambassador requested the use of B-52s, but that request was denied for several months.

The PAVN would not leave functioning outposts behind their advancing columns. LS 32 and LS 36, to the north and LS 02 to the south were also under siege conditions and holding on. The NVA planned to rout this PNK outpost and head west on Rt. 7 to re-assert their dominance of Military Region ll. They were poised for a blitzkrieg sweep across the PDJ. They knew the terrain well and planned to re-occupy their old haunts. They anticipated that the crushing loss of PNK would demoralize the five remaining Hmong hilltop outposts still overseeing the PDJ. They were bringing an overwhelming force of more than two Divisions to re-conquer the PDJ plateau and mountain caves.

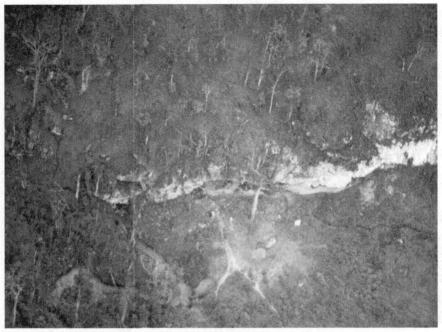

PAVN cave outpost, W. Platt collection

The NVA patiently waited for low ceilings and poor visibility to preclude airpower defense of the PNK outpost. Smoke and haze from dry season agricultural slash and burn fires lowered flight visibility and target acquisition.

This Rt.7 artery would be the primary corridor for the NVA drive to re-capture the PDJ.
BL could monitor the North Ban Ban Valley up to Rt. 6 toward Sam Neua, or down Rt. 7 southeast toward the infamous "Fishes Mouth" and Barthelemy pass. Twenty-five miles east was the Laos/ Vietnam border. BL was occasionally able to spot and target convoys. Russian trucks filled with NVA supplies flowed down this upper tentacle of the Ho Chi Minh Trail toward Saigon 800 miles south. A

first generation starlight scope was used for night perimeter observation and spotting road traffic in the valley below.

"Black Lion's outpost was the lonely keeper of this porous floodgate. These few men in foxholes were a festering thorn in the side of the NVA logistics net and military pride.

December 1969

The first week of December brought a four-day failed NVA assault on PNK.
Special NVA elements by-passed Phou Nok Kok and mounted a diversionary tank assault on Xieng Khouang City on 18 December 1969. Their attack on this provincial capital drew attention from a sapper attack of the Lima Lima airfield at LS22. Their objective was to destroy the heavy weapons and PT76 tanks stored beside the LL airfield. Enemy sappers breached the LL wire and blew up the many of the heavy weapons and tanks they abandoned during VP's "About Face" rout across the PDJ.

For the NVA, PNK was a symbolic node of resistance. She was perhaps, a beacon, a symbol of NVA retreat and humiliation. The mighty NVA had run like rats from the slaughter before VP's hardened, airborne guerilla fighters during "About Face." PAVN suffered a severe loss of territory and pride. This disgrace had to be avenged. It was a matter of prideful reprisal. The NVA soldiers absorbed heavy personnel losses. Leaders and Officers deemed the sacrifice necessary and acceptable.

During the three-month battle for PNK, USAF airstrikes killed and wounded thousands of front-line NVA soldiers around the PNK. The NVA had unlimited replacements and knew that VP did not. Attrition worked to their advantage. Ravens flying low level could reach the outpost but were often unable to direct airstrikes in the soup like smog blanketing the outposts.

The NVA counter-attack began at Phon Nok Kok. It would press west to capture both major PDJ runways, LS 22 and LS 108. First, they sweep west along Rt. 7 to Khang Khay and re-established a fortified base camp in the surrounding foothills. Battalion size units converged and prepared for their battle to take and hold the LL. They advanced southwest on Rt. 71 and Rt. 4 to Ban Ho on the southern PDJ. The Pathet Lao and PAVN planned a pincer movement to surround and destroy Sam Thong, LS 20 and Long Tieng, LS 20A before the spring rains.

Black Lion had one French 75 artillery piece and a recoilless rifle and a .50 cal machine gun to defend themselves. The NVA harassed them for continuously. Raven FACs and allied fighter aircraft functioned as long-range artillery. We located and attacked the NVA's truck parks and bulging stockpiles of war materials hidden in the Ban Ban valley. We destroyed hundreds of tons of NVA supplies with hundreds of air strikes in December 1969 and Janurary1970. Undaunted by heavy losses, the flood of fresh soldiers and war material continued moving toward their objectives.

Tom Harris, Raven 45, and I would hunt trucks and bulldozers together along Rt. 6 and 7 when other areas were covered with low clouds or fog. The hunt was usually a success when Tom and I teamed up. We would fly a loose, high-low, two-ship formation. One of us would search the road while the other kept a watch for ground-fire. One would brief inbound fighter flights while the other FAC directed bombers on the targets. We made a good team and trusted each other with our lives. Tom had my back, and I had his. We were brothers that shared the risks and fast tempo of war in MRll.

Greven collection

The northern section of the Ban Ban was a target rich environment as long convoys of equipment backed up north and east of Phon Nok Kok. We blew the tree canopy from above truck parks exposing petroleum (POL) tanks and ammo caches. Secondary explosions and black POL fires were the rewards for our sharp eyesight and low and slow flight. At that time, the Ban Ban valley was a free fire zone; so we did fire freely. When our marking rockets were expended, we would snake back to LL to re-arm, refuel, and catch our breath. Our, on the ground, turn-around time was about 15 minutes when fair weather, targets, and attack aircraft were available.

Upon Phon Nok Kok (PNK), sniper fire and incoming mortars pinned down the defenders. The enemy accuracy improved as they adjusted their aim. Then, sudden quiet for hours; but no one slept. Exhaustion overcame the defenders.

The NVA battle plan for this engagement was predictable Sun Tzu flavored Võ Nguyên Giáp strategy and tactics: isolate, restrict re-supply, exhaust, demoralize, and overpower the defenders.

Holding the PNK high ground indefinitely, against an overwhelming Army, was an improbable hope that faded as the PAVN's stranglehold tightened. They harassed ground patrols with snipers and ambush. A nearby road watch team was rescued while on the run. Within weeks, security patrols outside our wire ceased. The fighters were trapped in a deadly place far from home.

There were few Hmong personnel replacements for the wounded and dead. Decades of brutal conflict had culled a generation of young Hmong men. They fought with tenacity and courage against an overwhelmingly powerful and persistent North Vietnamese Army.

Harassment pressure became more frequent. Weeks of sleepless nights in rain-drenched foxholes wore down the defenders of Phon Nok Kok. The poor weather and visibility prevented airstrikes and critical re-supply as needed. The NVA plan was working. Harass the outpost, ambush patrols, and improve the trails that bypass the outposts.
Black Lion and the brave SGU officers and men waited for evacuation that could not, and did not, come. The hope was now for survival, one more hour, one more day.

RLAF AC-47 spooky gunships were tasked to patrol the PNK camp perimeter during the night when weather permitted. A-1 sky raiders patrolled the area and responded when the outpost was attacked at night.
Night gunship support increased as AC119's, some with heat sensors and side-looking radar, were employed. Flight crews remained on station all night spewing 7.62 and 20mm cannon fire on

maneuvering NVA squads that engaged the BL compound with crossfire tactics.

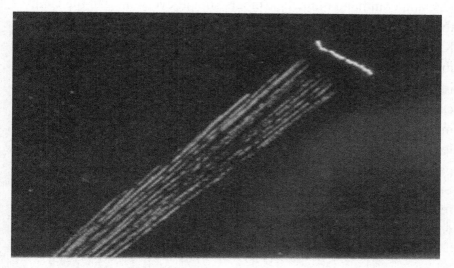

Spooky gunship, W. Platt collection

C 123, Greven collection

During daylight, hot re-supply landings by H-34s were often scuttled by intense ground fire. Enemy mortar teams zeroed in on the LZ, DZ, and command bunkers. Snipers shot at everything in the camp that moved. Sapper teams probed the perimeter wire while the King's men rolled grenades down the steep embankments toward them. Expended claymore mines could not always be replaced. Gaps in the wire now went un-repaired, Defenses weakened, and casualties increased. Air America C-47 and C-119 re-supply airdrop missions experienced heavy ground fire forcing them to fly higher, less accurate, airdrop altitudes. Occasionally the wind blew a critical parachute bundle across the drop zone to land in the hostile woods. Snipers fired on desperate troops scrambling from their foxholes to retrieve the bundles of food, water, and ammunition. Circling above, we few, saw the "Big Picture."

H 34, Greven collection

Some wounded could not be evacuated quickly, and reinforcements could not be delivered. Medical supplies were running low and the body bags of friends ripened in the sun. Thru interconnecting trench lines fighters would run the gantlet for water, food, ammunition, and latrine facilities. The site was now an impotent impact zone.

Defenders stayed alert for a pending assault while convoys of regular NVA poured through the Rt.7 choke point toward the PDJ.

Sapper units breached the wire many nights. Hand to hand combat ensued, and the sappers were again repelled. Snipers fired on everything that moved in, or over, the camp. An occasional helicopter got in with a few replacements and took out the critically wounded before mortars slammed into the LZ as they departed. Whump!

January 8, 1970

Today, the wounded could not be evacuated; medical supplies and body bags were not available. The battered warriors were exhausted. They hunkered down; weakened, yet still a fighting force.

January 9, 1970

A few Ravens were able to sneak under the cloud deck, weave through mountain passes, and reach the Black Lion outpost. Just the sight and sound of our aircraft overhead may have dissuaded enemy attack. Our presence may have boosted our soldier's morale for an instant. We would fire our rockets at tree lines and fire our AR 15's rifles out the window toward suspected sniper positions trying to draw attention to ourselves and provide respite for weary soldiers. We patrolled and circled the camp drawing fire until fuel was low. Then we had to go. Leaving them was bitter sorrow. We did all that we could. It was never enough.

As the situation worsened, Ambassador Godley mandated that CAS officers return to Long Tieng at night. Reluctant, angry, and frustrated, Will Green complied and left his troops on the hill, maybe to die without him. Tough men agonize for brave friends left behind.

Cornered, out-numbered, out-gunned, and dying in the mud was a horrifying scenario for us to digest.

January 10, 1970.

Now, out of resources, our exhausted fighters chose survival over death. They hung tough as long as possible. On the night of Jan 10, 1970, they bolted off the high ground and down west into the forest. They escaped and evaded most enemy patrols on the 25-mile gantlet back to the momentary safe harbor of LS 22. Many Hmong soldiers did not survive that hostile trek. Good men were lost because evacuations were planned too late to execute during fair weather.

We each left a piece of our innocence on that bloodstained mountain. For me, Phon Nok Kok is a mountain shrine to the spirit of courage; limestone evidence of life's fragility. We awoke again before dawn to find and support the remnant, if possible.

American pilots, crews, support personnel, and CIA field officers mentally shared the PNK soldier's daily ordeal. By night, we had warm food, a cold beer, a cool shower, and a soft, clean, bed. Our SGU brothers rested in the dirt, behind enemy lines. I prayed for their safety and our courage. There were whispers in the dark to our family at home, "I love you!"

January 13, 1970, (my 25th Birthday)

The NVA broke the chokehold of Rt.7 with the fall of the "Black Lion" outpost on Mount Phon Nok Kok. The floodgates were open; bumper to bumper PAVN trucks, tanks, and fresh artillery rolled west on Highway 7 toward the 7/71 split and Khang Khay. Masked by smoke, haze, and overcast ceilings, they re-established their bunkered hideouts, camouflaged truck parks, and buried storage areas. The full array of PAVN anti-aircraft guns flanked the one and a half lane highway. These guns were mobile and methodically protected the columned convoy of men and material as they advanced. Concentrations developed at strategic travel intervals, stream crossings, and cave-riddled escarpments. Anti-aircraft batteries now fiercely guarded the major roads and storage infrastructure. The NVA cleared the road ahead with armored vehicles and infantry.

Diving through sucker holes and screaming along-side Rt.7 below the clouds was trolling for trouble. Ravens did it to find targets. As the weather cleared, I was ready with targets to destroy. The first FAC, who found a good and workable target, controlled the available fighter sorties. It was competition for best BDA and mission of the day. Each pilot had his own technique for finding good targets and staying alive. We all believed our skills were the best, of the best. We smiled and drank in appreciation of each other's success and bravado. We were a reckless mini-squadron of serious scouts looking to bomb and burn the enemy shooting at us or our friends. Destroying enemy weapons, food, material, and gasoline was our mission and duty.

Greven collection

Chapter 10

https://www.wep11345.com/chapter-10-.html

PAVN Headquarters

***The two most powerful warriors are patience and time.
-Leo Tolstoy***

PAVN Nong Pet Stronghold, 1970, W. Platt collection

15 January 1970

Then, on a distant hill, we spotted a sign to investigate. A wispy column of gray smoke gently climbed the horizon.

"Raven, go to the low. Enemy."

Yang Bee's arm rested on my shoulder as he pointed northeast, and glassed the valley trail 800ft below.

"Many enemy, No Friend here. Call Fighters, many trucks, many NVA. We Kill!"

Scout translator, warrior, Yang Bee,
had the eyes of an eagle to see,
His enemies run from his Hmong gun,
VP's chief "Robin" scout was he.

I took a deep breath to speak clear and slow. We separate from the target area to gain altitude and provide a briefing to inbound A-1 fighter aircraft.

"Copy FireFly, CBU 24, Mark 84s, and strafe."

"You will be cleared random headings, multiple passes."

"The Ceiling is 1,200ft broken and clearing. The latest altimeter is 29.89. I will climb on top, rendezvous with you and lead you to the target. Tally Ho!"

"You see Bunkers on both sides of the ridgeline; a smoldering troop encampment is under the gray smoke on top. Looks to me like a breakfast fire gone wrong. Hit that smoke on your first pass."

"In the ravine under the low trees and bushes are bunkers. Trucks are in the tree lines by the rice paddies to the north. I say again, small arms anticipated; no larger weapons observed but very possible."

Greven collection

"Please save some 20mm cannon to cover my post strike, Bomb Damage Assessment (BDA). Tell me what you see on your run-in. Good Luck. Smoke is away."
Raven, FireFly 31 lead, "we have you and your smoke in sight."

"CLEARED HOT"! FireFly

"Hit my smoke."

"Lead is in from the northeast...exit to the West."

"Guns on the left, tracers on the right, troops in the open, fight, fight, fight."

"Two is in Hot from the east with a north departure. FAC and Lead are in sight."

"Tally-Ho. Hit my smoke! CLEARED HOT!" said I.

Greven collection

A1, 1969, W. Platt collection

Chapter 11

https://www.wep11345.com/chapter-11.html

PT-76 Tank Attack

Do not swallow bait offered by the enemy.
-Sun Tzu

PT 76 Tanks, Flack Trap, 1970, W. Platt collection

In late January 1970, the NVA set a PT 76 Tank carcass in the middle of Rt. 7 about four miles east of the entrance to the Ban Ban Valley. The Tank was just north of our forward position on Phou Nok Kok. What a great target. I made a low pass and snapped a photograph.

Somehow, this target did not look or feel right; too easy, too conspicuous.

Was this Tank being repaired?

The engine cover was removed, and a track was off one side. The opportunity to direct an airstrike on a tank was exciting. I first located it while scanning Rt. 7 with my field glasses. I reported my location to "Cricket" who began to find available fighters with the right ordinance on to destroy the tank. I descended to about 700 feet out of sight of the tank and readied my 35mm, Asai Pentax, camera to capture this handsome target. My windows were open, and my right hand held my camera. My left hand was on the stick as I kicked opposite rudder and adjusted the trim with camera in hand.

Now I needed to see if any gunners were defending that tank. Threat information is critical to fighter pilots planning their ordinance delivery and altitude release parameters.
Somehow, this target did not look or feel right; too easy, too conspicuous.

I banked hard left, snapped the photograph out my left window, and there they were; in my face. Long-barreled anti-aircraft weapons protruded from several bunkers on each side of the road. Initially, they were all aimed east down Rt. 7 to my seven o'clock.

The NVA camo-nets over the guns were obvious and deep bunkers were plainly visible on both sides of the road. Maybe too late, I realized this was a dangerous target with bite; a flack-trap. With a last glance, I saw a second tank and several guns tracking me.

Was a prolonged look at these targets worth my life, or those of fighter pilots?
No, Not today. I saw what I needed to see; now, I want out of here.

Two 12.7 or 14.5 Anti-Aircraft weapons were rotating in my direction. They wanted to track and lead my progress through the gorge for an easy kill.

I was doing 120 KIAS and diving for speed. My eventual pull up just about ripped the wings clean off my O-1 Birddog. I zoomed and only gained six hundred feet of altitude and suffered a loss of airspeed back L/D max. I kicked rudder and jinked for my life. Then I dove for speed again. This time, it was essential to be well un-coordinated and fly like a twisting purple martin.

White and green tracers flashed by both sides of my canopy. My windows were open, and the sound of popcorn made me get "TINY" in the cockpit. (Thus my nickname "Tiny") Time stopped, and I was frozen in the mental slow-motion of escape. It was like wanting to run and not able to move my legs.

The tracers were passing further away now as I praised God for deliverance and then composed my pucker. This was one flak trap that almost got me. There would be several more.

I took a deep breath, the first one in 45 seconds. I calmed my spirit and reported the trap and guns to ABCCC. My voice was a few octaves higher, but my speech was "Cool Operator."

The Airborne command and control C130 was orbiting at altitude, 60 miles to the south, They did not have fighters available.

"Come back later Raven 43. We will find you some fighters."

'Rodger, 43 is RTB LS22. Will report LL in sight, over and out for now.'

From a standoff range of about 2 miles, I lobbed, then adjusted all eight Willy Pete rockets into the NVA perimeter and headed for LS 22. Time to re-arm my bird, eat an MRE lunch, drink water, lots of water, and have a stretch. I pondered the tactics of the hunter and the hunted as I ate.

Three days later, we finished the work, but it took 24 fighter sorties to kill the tank and guns. We did not lose an aircraft through a few fighters took small arms hits. It was a good fight with a good outcome. Everyone earned their keep, and the NVA got a well-deserved nose job.

PAVN outpost Rt 71, 1970, W. Platt collection

Chapter 12

https://www.wep11345.com/chapter-12-.html

PAVN at the 7/71 Split

We are not fit to lead an army on the march unless we are familiar with the face of the country--its mountains and forests, its pitfalls and precipices, its marshes and swamps.
-Sun Tzu

Highways 7 and 71 split at Nong Pet, W. Platt collection

The junction of Rt. 7 and Rt. 71 at Nong Pet points northeast toward Phon Nok Kok and the Ban Ban valley. The PAVN defended this intersection with anti-aircraft weapons as armored convoys rolled west on Rt.71 toward Kang Khay and Rt.74. One division of the determined PAVN juggernaut flowed southwest on Rt.7 and Rt. 4 to

Xieng Khouang, LS03, and the LS22 Airfield we called LL. They pincered LL until it fell and then they headed west for Mong Soui. It was a blitzkrieg offensive spreading across the PDJ travel corridors. Our five Hmong hilltop outposts around the PDJ were evacuated under direct pressure from a numerically smothering onslaught of olive drab soldiers. The NVA dispersion along strategic routes neared completion. Their headquarter concentrations were few, far between, well disguised and guarded by AAA.

They paused to regroup for a week. Then they pushed southwest toward the mountains and our newly constituted Vang Pao Line defending Long Tieng and Sam Thong.

Methodically the PAVN spread like ants west along dirt roads and the Nam Ngum river tributaries. Ravens successfully found and bombarded platoon-sized enemy elements but were met by rings of 37mm AAA protecting truck park assets and Battalion sized units of NVA and PL.

Guns, tracers, and narrow escapes kept our vulnerable, aircraft at standoff distances. Serious gunners now had ample ammunition to fire on any aircraft within range. Their aggressiveness hindered our target acquisition and bombing effectiveness. We struck from a standoff distance, and assessment of bomb damage in the target area often had to be made through binoculars; the ground fire was very thick.

Diving through sucker holes, then bobbing and weaving across dirt roads and streams were trolling for trouble. Ravens did it to find quality targets. As the weather cleared, we had several targets identified for destruction. When jet bombers could work in existing weather conditions, we struck hard and fast. Our fighters were often Bingo fuel as they were diverted from other missions to strike our targets.

"We are low on fuel Raven; we will drop all of our bombs on the first pass. Over".

"Rodger Hit My Smoke." The mass of explosions sounded like thunder and destroyed everything within 100 yards of impact.

Ravens FACs had an ongoing competition for the best BDA, of the day. (Bomb Damage Assessment) The first Raven FAC locating a workable target claimed the first fighter sorties available from Cricket. (ABCCC, Airborne Command, Control, and Communications)

Each Raven developed his technique for finding good targets and staying alive. We all believed that our techniques, skills, and judgment could foil the gunner's plan. If I am still in one piece, I must be doing something right. If you are taking hits or seeing tracers, it is time to change tactics.

Being an elusive target was a constant effort. Continuous changes in pitch, bank, and roll proved most effective for me. The lower my altitude, the more intentionally radical my flight path, altitude, and airspeed became. I could flip every switch without looking and flew my craft with ambidextrous hands, elbows, knees, and feet. My neck was a swivel; my 20/15 eyes sight focused on un-natural clues. Straight lines, circles, and right angles are humanmade. Fake arrays of vegetation, odd shapes, and subtle colors differences were obvious camouflage. Trails show signs of travel, and fresh tracks of matted grass led to hideouts, bunkers, trenches, and caves. Recent digs of orange dirt or helmet reflections in the sun would catch my attention and ire. "We were just boys playing tag with gunners" Our SGU's played the old game of "King of the Mountain with grenades and guns rather than dirt balls and water balloons." Some youthful play trained cagy warriors.

Chapter 13

https://www.wep11345.com/chapter-13.html

Fortress Khang Khay

You must not fight too often with one enemy, or you will teach him all your art of war.
-N. Bonaparte

Kang Khay, Road Runner lake, Rt.7, 1969, Greven collection

Chinese cultural center, Khang Khay, Rt. 7, W. Platt collection

30 January 1970

After the fall of Phon Nok Kok, NVA convoys rolled west through the 7/71 split to re-occupy the PDJ. The PAVN lead elements dashed to the well-defended sanctuary near Khang Khay and dug in. This stretch along Rt.71 was the most dangerous area on the PDJ. It sheltered major supply depots and large caves. The nine-level gunners defended this stronghold with purpose and courage.

Ravens were prohibited from striking within five miles of the Chinese Cultural Center (CCC) at Khang Khay. This strategic area contained old French outposts dating back to the French colonial days and American forts constructed in the 1950's.

Now the NVA re-occupied their old defensive positions and re-stocked their storage bunkers, ammo dumps, and POL facilities. This area near Khang Khay became a stronghold and logistics hub from which to launch and support attacks on RLA, Thai, and Hmong PDJ outposts. Our "Rules of Engagement" gave the enemy a safe-haven from which to operate. They stored their military material in the Cultural Center and near the Buddhist temple. These facilities were not targeted while I was there.

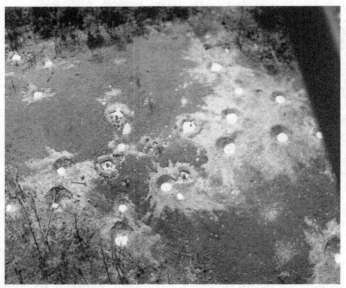

AAA, PDJ, Rt.71, 1970, W. Platt collection

Mobile 2-ZPU, PDJ, 1970 W. Platt collection

Chapter 14

https://www.wep11345.com/chapter-14.html

Fall of LS 22 Airfield

Hence to fight and conquer in all your battles is not supreme excellence; supreme excellence consists in breaking the enemy's resistance without fighting.
-Sun Tzu

LS22, LL, W. Platt collection

8 February 1970,

North Vietnam's 144th Regiment attacked the airstrip of Xieng Khouang village (L-03) which Vang Pao had captured in April 69.

PDJ, LL, Greven collection

Since then this strategically located, central PDJ runway and defensive positions had been available to Raven O1's, T-28s, and cargo aircraft. For the next ten days, 6,000 or more North Vietnamese troops attacked SGU positions along Route 7. They gathered for the main siege and assault on Xieng Khouang's compounds and aviation facilities.

LL, Greven collection

Their objective now was to reclaim and occupy the airfield and fortress firebase at LS22. (LL)

Enemy Scouting parties set ambushes for LL patrols and established lookout posts keeping 24/7 eyeballs on LL activities. Their observation posts soon became mortar positions and fire control elements. North of LS22, NVA long-range artillery was positioned to zero in on the airfield runway and ramp. 122mm rocket launchers slammed explosives into the LS22 airfield defensive compounds. Small squads of sappers tested the camp defenses following intermittent shelling sprees. Snipers shot from well-concealed positions and kept the defenders on high alert. Our allied artillery batteries returned proximity fire without locating specific targets.

Ravens located and bombarded squad sized lead elements of NVA units but rarely found larger concentrations of force. Ground-fire intensified as we worked north of LL. The jets and we were obliged to fly and fight from higher altitudes and hopefully out of range.

Soon the LL defenders were exhausted. They fought hard while leaders planned an orderly withdrawal. The weather cleared momentarily, and Ravens found and destroyed small-dispersed targets but were unable to locate the long-range artillery that now hammered the LL Airfield. Mortar rounds landed close to Air America planes as they made resupply and evacuation flights.

Ambassador Godley withdrew American advisory personnel from LS22 at dusk and returned them at daybreak. We despised that lack of resolve and loyalty to our Hmong allies. Ambassador Godley was under extreme pressure to minimize the further loss of American lives in Laos.

PDJ, Rt. 7, 1969 Garrity collection

Chapter 15

https://www.wep11345.com/chapter-15.html

B52 Arc-light PDJ

The problem in defense is how far you can go without destroying from within what you are trying to defend from without.
-Dwight D. Eisenhower

First PDJ Arc-light, W. Platt collection

February 18, 1970

Nighttime, B52 arc-light missions began on the southern PDJ just 20 miles south, of our airfield at LL. The entire valley rumbled and shook the souls of soldier and civilians on both sides of the conflict. In the first hours of February 18, 1970, B-52 arc light strikes pounded the southern PDJ for the first time. The rapid PAVN advance to the Southern PDJ and the Vang Pao Line forewarned of a siege of Sam Tong and Long Tieng. Unknown to Ravens, the Ambassador had upped the weapons ante by carpet-bombing the mountains and valleys overlooking the southern PDJ. As for accuracy, it was true that all of the bombs hit the ground. February 20, 1970.

Demoralized, isolated, and spooked, our troops vacated their defensive positions. LL was abandoned to the enemy along with a large cache of military supplies and equipment. We lost our emergency landing and refueling airfield in the middle of the PDJ. Our soldiers skillfully avoided enemy ambush, and most units straggled into Sam Thong and Long Tieng weeks later.

In all of February, there were only 13 days of good airstrike weather. The NVA used the bad weather to move and fortify their web of positions on the PDJ. A pall of smoke and haze hung over the region. The flight visibility was less than three miles and lasted for a week at a time. The smoke layer thinned for a few days and then thickened again. Above eight thousand feet, the visibility would be 10 miles or more but looking down I could not see the ground through the smoke. It was a sea of misty gray.

21 February 1970

Three-thousand, North Vietnamese soldiers assaulted Xieng Khouangville and successfully overran allied defenses. Most of the Hmong defenders escaped to rejoin General Vang Pao's SGUs near LS 72.

Chapter 16

https://www.wep11345.com/chapter-16-.html

Mong Soui Abandon

So in war, the way is to avoid what is strong and to strike at what is weak.
-Sun Tzu

LS108 Mong Soui, W. Platt collection

25 February 1970.

North Vietnamese snipers began harassing Mong Suoi patrols.

27 February 1970

LS 108 Airfield falls quickly to communist forces. Laotian neutralists defending Mong Soui abandon their positions with the first harassing attack. The FAN security simply dissolved. The long dirt Airfield there was a major staging base for Thai and RLAF T-28 aircraft supporting FAR and Thai forces patrolling the northwest PDJ. As Mong Soui falls, the number of airstrike sorties flown in support of the VP line of defense decreases. The L20A Hmong stronghold, the refugee center and hospital at LS 20, Sam Tong were now threatened. The NVA occupation of the PDJ plateau was complete. The mountains delayed the NVA advance.

Fighting slowed for a few weeks due to weather challenges and reconstitution of forces. The NVA prepared their attack and hand carried supplies and arms up the limestone paths to their forward units approaching the eastern end of Skyline Ridge. They fortified their positions near Khang Kho and Phou Khe on the southern PDJ and prime targets for frequent B52, arc light, carpet-bombing missions. The PAVN losses were severe, but they absorbed them and continued to push up the steep incline toward the prizes of San Tong and Long Tieng.

General Vang Pao established a defensive line where the mountains met the PDJ. LS 72, Tha Tam Bleung, LS 15, Ban Na, and Sala Phou Khoun became strongholds containing the bulk of Hmong and RLA SGU defenders.

28 February 1970

Twenty Thai pilots and their aircraft now flew daily airstrike operations from Udorn RTAFB. RLAF T28s cycled each morning from Vientiane and Udorn to the battle areas. Ban Na (LS15) and LS 249 replaced Mong Soui as the forward operating locations for refueling and re-armament the T28s.

6 March 1970

PAVN units occupied all former Hmong outposts around the PDJ. They had stormed south on the eastern side of the Nam Ngum to within 5 miles of Sam Tong, LS20. Some elite enemy units bypassed LS 72 and LS15 while others pinned down SGUs within their bunkered perimeters. Several FAR positions on the south edge of the PDJ were withdrawn to fortify ridgelines closer to LS 20A.

Pres Nixon spoke on American involvement in Laos. He stated that no US personnel in Laos were killed in ground combat operations there. In fact, seven Americans had lost their lives at LS 85 in 1968; another ambush had killed several USAID workers at forward villages.

L20A, children, 1970, W. Platt collection

Chapter 17

https://www.wep11345.com/chapter-17.html

Freedom Highway

It is a military axiom not to advance uphill against the enemy, nor to oppose him when he comes downhill. -Sun Tzu

Skyline Ridge defenders February 1970, W. Platt collection

During an afternoon weather pause, Weird Harold Masaris and I covertly commandeered a white maintenance jeep and escaped the fortress valley for a few hours of sightseeing exploration. Armed and ready we drove toward the awesome Skyline Ridge towering 1200 feet above us. We locked the hubs in four-wheel drive and tied down the cooler filled with cokes, ice and Hershey bars. We brought refreshment gifts for the children and Hmong soldiers we chanced to meet.

The adventure commenced with a toast to long life. We traveled the bumpy single lane dirt road northwest from Long Tieng toward Sam Tong. A line of modest Hmong Farms and defensive bunkers thinned out, and the mountain flowed cool water from the side of a limestone cliff. A water truck was positioned beside the small waterfall. A group of men filled the tank with spring water to distribute to the tens of thousands of thirsty defenders and their families sheltered in the fortress valley to our east. A team of women washed laundry downstream. Everyone had chores to do and worked for the common good of all.

We began the long switchback climb up the limestone face of freedom highway. There was no turning back, no shoulder, no stopping, and no options but go forward or fall. We pressed ahead. The jeep's four tires were spiting yellow dust and light gravel as we clawed for traction up the ominous slope. Weird looked at me and shook his head in playful amazement at the 15-degree ascent ahead. Harold was hanging over the edge hoping I was as skillful as I was confident. Like our General Vang Pao, the stubborn, proud jeep climbed the treacherous path up the face of fate. The road zinged, sagged and struggled for the pinnacle. Up we went coaxing momentum to the top. There was a fork in the path, and we took it. We made a right turn onto the trail leading east along Skyline drive toward our communication towers and Tacan station channel 98.

We stopped at the first sentry outpost. It was ringed with meager barbed wire and deep trenches. There were a few huts and bunkers cut into the rounded north face of the ridge. Mortars and machine guns pointed northeast down Freedom's Highway toward Sam Tong 15 miles away. A five-man Hmong squad with rifles, hand grenades, and handheld communications radio secured the entrance to Skyline Ridge and the trail back down into our Long Tieng valley.

The squad leader, Tua, greeted us with a sharp salute and the welcome of a brother coming home from a long journey. We acted like airplanes until they understood we were Ravens.

"They know who we are; I buzz their bunkers often and airdrop candy and gum."

We were given the short tour of the site and then shared cokes, smiles, and handshakes. The bond of goodwill was solidified in frozen chocolate.

Our Hmong sentries, lined up for a photograph and a few Hmong wives emerged from the bunkers to join their men. The work was never ending on these picket outposts. Food, water, fire, and supplies needed constant attention. The floor and walls were packed earth. A few bags of rice, a pot of boiling water over the campfire, and a large domestic pig was waiting for dinner. Life on the ridge above Long Tieng was basic survival and constant alert. War, this close to home, is a family affair. Home is the final fighting position. Family and friends are protected to the last breath.

A teacher said, "Life is suffering, loss, and grief. Everyone gets a piece of the grief." How we deal with tragedy and hardship is a matter of love and compassion, or, anger and hate. One choice is renewed life, and one is enduring, dark, destructive pain. The reality is that we will grieve forever. We will not get over the loss of a loved one; we will learn to live with it. We will heal and rebuild our self around the loss we have suffered. We will be whole again. We will never be the same nor will we want to be.

I mentioned to Harold that I noted the presence of Montagnard women in the trenches around Bu Prang Special Forces camp A236 in South Vietnam when I was a ground FAC there. Family nurses were needed when the fighting was fierce. Women fired weapons when death was near. "Given no place to run or hide we all fight like Alamonians"; Weird Harold quipped in irony.

These bunkers had overhead cover for protection from the natural elements. One bunker had an earth roof. High flying mortars, distant snipers, and long-range rocket-propelled-grenades could destroy an outpost given enough time.

"I heard Jerry say that 12,000 NVA soldiers are trekking our way. Currently, NVA scouts are observing Sam Tong. That is less than twenty miles that way."

"Yes, do you have any more good news?"
"Yes, we will not have to fly so far to find them."

" Right!"

We drove the crest of Skyline Ridge and marveled at the jagged horizon of mountains and valleys stretching northeast to the Plaines de Jarres. Here they come! Right!

"Do you think our Vang Pao Line of defense will collapse to this Ridgeline?"

"I do!"

"This ridge looks like towering castle walls and ramparts surrounding a European medieval mountain fortress."

LS 20A, 1970, W. Platt collection

"Or, Dien Bien Phu?"

"Right!"

"Classic Sun Tzu," I said.

" Who?"

"Sun Tzu!" the 5th century BC Chinese General, who wrote the book.

"The Art of War," I said.

"Man, this war is some very ugly art!"

"Right."

"Remember when Churchill read Hitler's Mein Kamph?"

" Right!"

" I recall that General Patton read the tactics manual authored by the German General Rommel."

"Right!" "What is your point?"

"Never mind!" The Sun TZU is going down; we had better head back down to the valley."

" Right!"

Long Tieng market, Buddhist temple, 1970, W. Platt collection

Garrity collection

Garrity collection

Chapter 18

https://www.wep11345.com/chapter-18.html

Refugees Attacked at Sam Tong

When you surround an army, leave an outlet free. Do not press a desperate foe too hard. -Sun Tzu

LS 20 Sam Tong, March 1970, W. Platt collection

12 March 1970

Air America aircraft evacuated hundreds of patients from the refugee hospital at Sam Thong to safe locations. USAID workers, CIA advisors, and US attachés were transported to Long Tieng. "Pop" Buell, was evacuated by helicopter just hours before PAVN soldiers overran the airstrip. The hospital and many buildings were burned to the ground. Tens of thousands of Hmong women, children, and elderly villagers fled the refugee center and walked quickly down freedom Highway to toward Long Tieng. Most arrived safely, and the non-combatant refugees were flown to refugee settlements further south. VP kept his key clan leaders, SGU's, and their families there in Long Tieng with him. Our valley was large and currently held more than 20,000 souls. The NVA hit the VP Line and by-passed major conflict until they reached LS 20, Sam Tong.

16 March 1970

LS 72, Tha Tam Bleung, was evacuated.

17 March 1970

General Vang Pao recalled all SGU's from the VP line to fortify LS20A.
The Royal Thai Army (RTA) sent a 700 men regimental combat team and three more howitzers to 20A. RLA SGU's from MRlll and MR IV arrive to help defend LS 20A. Thai 105 and 155mm howitzer batteries settled on the south and west rim of the valley. The fighting reached Skyline ridge many times and was repulsed. Continuous Artillery and T 28 bombardment held off the major PAVN assault. The NVA hid artillery spotters where they could see and adjust the impact zone accuracy of their long-range artillery and 122mm rockets. The night defense included USAF A-1 Sky Raiders, AC-47, AC-119, and AC.130 gunships. They riddled the NVA advances with volleys of accurate firepower.

LS 72, Tha Tam Bleung, VP Line, 1970, W. Platt collection

LS 16, Vang Vieng, 1970, William E. Platt collection

Chapter 19

https://www.wep11345.com/chapter-19.html

Skyline Ridge Artillery spotters

The enemy's spies who have come to spy on us must be sought out.
-Sun Tzu

Skyline Ridge, 1970, W. Platt collection

18 March 1970

Elements of the PAVN 312th division were approaching Long Tieng. Sappers infiltrated Long Tieng's security perimeter and bypassed some sentries last night. Sapper commandos carrying explosive satchel charges were intercepted and killed before they reached the flight line.

A 122mm rocket destroyed a Raven O-1, and a nearby Hmong soldier was severely wounded. Mortars and rockets had impacted the L 20A airfield flight line for several nights, and the possibility of a full assault on the airfield loomed as a distinct possibility. We Ravens were prepared to defend ourselves from infiltrators if necessary. Our building became a bunker. We each had our favorite weapons ready for action.

In my spare canvas map bag, I had four hand-grenades, six M79 rounds, 100 rounds of .38 caliber red tracer, six 20 round magazines of 5.56 x 45, 62 grain, red tip tracer ammunition. That forty-pound sack of explosives was "personal equipment" that flew with me every mission. My M-79 grenade launcher strapped onto my map bag. My Colt AR-15 assault rifle had a foldable stock and green shoulder strap. He weighed about 10 lbs loaded with twin twenty cartridge magazines taped together. He was only 33.6 in tall, and the his15-inch barrel was tipped with a conical flash suppressor. My combat masterpiece pistol was a blued Smith and Wesson 38 special loaded with five tracer rounds and a single round of ball and jacket under the hammer. On the way home most days, I would visit the hump gunner's pit, an area where I drew ground fire several times. The PL initiated ground-fire and always missed. I would deliver a stream of full automatic red tracer from my AR 15 every day I flew. With a muzzle velocity of 3000fps, I could walk my tracers on to a small target area. To become effective operating an automatic weapon out the side window of a light airplane, one must practice often. It seemed only fair to deliver a counter-attack whenever possible. Back on the ground, I cleaned the weapons after every use.

Jerry Rhein took me aside and briefed me on the need to find and destroy an enemy artillery spotter off the departure end of the Long Tieng runway.

"They must be well-concealed and dug in somewhere along Skyline's eastern ridge." Jerry said.

Flying with Yang Bee (VB) was always eventful. He had a reputation for aggressive behavior in our rear seat. Shooting out the window to announce his presence was a gantlet thrown by a bad, mad Hmong.

At first light, Yang Bee was waiting for me. He nodded, and I gave him a salute and thumbs up. While I pre-flighted the O-1, he opened the rear seat side windows and prepared his AK 47 assault rifle and ammunition magazines for combat. He wedged the weapon in beside his seat. I had flown with him on several previous occasions. I knew him to be fearless, and he expected me to follow his instructions without hesitation. He barked over the intercom, "Raven 43, "go to the Low," which, from experience, I knew he meant to hug the terrain and prepare to fight, and, maybe die.

Bee Yang was a legendary figure and a fierce warrior who was a trusted confidant of General Vang Pao. His appearance and demeanor reminded me of a veteran drill instructor. He was a coiled and tempered spring ready to attack. This mission would be another test of survivability. We would fly and fight Low and Slow until we found the hidden NVA artillery spotter.
My chief crew, Glen held up a sign that read "No Fly, No die"; morbid humor, he said, wards off the superstitious jinx.

Within minutes after takeoff, we were in a hard left bank turn around the jagged karsts and grassy knolls that formed the eastern edge of Skyline Ridge. Level with the ridge and flying 200 feet laterally, we followed the contour up and focused on specific locations with a concealed view of the Long Tieng valley to the west. Just below us was a nearly vertical ridge falling 1500 feet down a canyon wall. Suddenly, we both saw three olive-drab enemy artillery spotters, scurrying into their spider holes. Swinging their assault rifles toward us, Vang Bee opened up with full automatic fire out his rear left side window. I hoped he would not sever our left wing strut. Our O1 was still climbing at 70 KIAs toward an overcast layer a few hundred feet above us. Time stopped, I held my breath. Knowing that there were rocks in those clouds ahead, I pulled a hard right 270 with a hard-left 90 turn back east alongside the ridge. By the time I rolled out, Vang Bee was firing out the right rear window at the burrowing bad guys. My ears were ringing near pain inside my ballistic helmet as VB discharged his third complete magazine volley at the enemy. The ceiling was too low to work fighters, so we popped the ridge and entered final approach for 32 at L 20A. VB briefed VP by radio on the exact location of the NVA artillery spotters. We landed, and within minutes, a truck full of Hmong fighters was dispatched to the eastern ridge to clear the remaining spotters from their lair. This was just another exciting flight with Master Warrior scout Yang Bee.

Vang Pao's counter-offensive was able to drive back the invaders and to re-claim Sam Tong by the end of March 1970.

Hmong Trench warfare, Garrity collection

Hmong Family Bunker 1970, Garrity collection

Chapter 20

https://www.wep11345.com/chapter-20.html

Freedom is not Free

In war, there are no unwounded soldiers.
-José Narosky

37mm Anti Aircraft Artillery, Rt. 71 March 1970, W. Platt collection

26 March 1970

Raven FACs Henry Allen and Dick Elzinga disappeared in route from Vientiane to Long Tieng. We expected them to walk out of the mountains and greet us with great survival stories. They were not heard from again. We searched every mountain pass and riverbed for a sign of their crash site or survival markers. We found nothing. Our morale bottomed out. Now we felt the pain; the loss of friends. Time to gather our strength and continue the fight.

The PAVN had secured the entire PDJ, and our airstrikes were now brutal payback for friends lost. The daily battles continued as new Ravens replaced the fallen ones.

24 April 1970

On a rare fair weather day, Jim Cross, an MRV Raven, loaded up a new, first flight Raven, Dave Reese. It started out as a positioning Flight to 20A. Both men died in a 37mm shoot down of their U-17B near the Ban Ban Valley western wall. That was their first and last combat mission in MRll. Why they ventured near the deadly Ban Ban, 40 miles east-northeast of 20A, I could not imagine and do not speculate. Both men were experienced SVN FACs, but neither man was an experienced survivor in the deadly MRll anti-aircraft-artillery environment. I was sure that decisions made were well intended and seemed reasonable. It was not productive or necessary to second-guess lost men and senior warriors. We just accepted that everyone did the best they could at the time. Then with a tear and prayer, we moved on to the dangers of the daily mission. The reality of lost friends was eternalized, never to be forgotten. I experienced the haunting need for faith and grace that sustains us all in the worst of times. The mission came first, and we continued fighting with the hope that a miracle would spare the brave Hmong people and us.

The men I flew with as Ravens were warriors who understood the risks and price of war.

We were all volunteers who relied on each other for survival and encouragement in the deadly MRll environment. We fought behind the enemy front lines and attacked his infrastructure with ferocity and accuracy. We believed that our Laotian, Cambodian, and Thai allies deserved an opportunity for freedom from communist oppression. Our government leaders looked to disengage. MRll was merely a holding action during another American Skedaddle. All gave some; some gave all. We will remember the tens of thousands of honorable men from many nations who fought and died for another man's freedom.

We all did our best for a cause we believed important. Sky officers like Tom Clines, Jerry Daniels, and Hugh Tovar advised, encouraged, and supplied General Vang Pao. Frontline SGU advisors like Jim Adkins and Will Green led with courage and distinction. Air America and Continental Air service pilots like Lee Gossett, and John Wiren and their flight crews worked tirelessly to accomplish their humanitarian and hard rice missions. They frequently rescued downed Ravens and fighter pilots from enemy capture. The risks were high, and the rewards unheralded and personal. Our support system included tens of thousands of Americans service personnel and allies who contributed their all to freedom's cause in MRll. Our teamwork and fortitude were spent without the reward and vindication of victory.

Among the selfless heroes of history's conflicts are the Hmong Pilots, Soldiers, Women, and their innocent children. Their spirit of courage endured the carnage, misery, separation, and sacrifice of war. Hmong women and soldiers saved their timeless communal culture of ancestral clans, family traditions, and values. They suffered for Freedom. The cost was family grief.

With US Embassy advice and responsibility, the Hmong fought our enemy and lost 40,000 young men on our mutual behalf. The lives of more than one hundred thousand women, children, and elderly were ripped apart by evacuation and dependence on aid. US intentions were probably honorable, but the consequences of our policy shattered an ancient way of life and resulted in great suffering by innocent civilians. Superpower treaties did not consider or prioritize the long-term care of people caught in the crossfire of ideologies. Enforcement of Super Power agreements by the International Control Commission (ICC) was inept and invited gross violations that produced the Secret War in Laos.

In 1973, we abandoned loyal allies to fight on with meager support and hope. Within two years, the Royal government fell to the communist factions who hunted down the remnant Hmong soldiers for extermination. Chased to the Mekong River, the surviving Hmong found poverty refuge in Thailand camps. Eventually, some Hmong families became immigrants to various countries including the USA. Despite the hardships of diaspora and assimilation, they persevered.

As third generation Hmong-American citizens thrive in America, We remember their steadfastness against the storm of communism. The price of countering communist expansion and defending another man's freedom became too high for US citizens to bear. They rallied in mass protests and demanded that their representatives get our boys out of SEA. Americans did not consider the consequences and horror of more war on innocent civilians. We abandoned friends and allies to un-fathomable brutality. Their sacrifice is remembered. Discarded agreements with allies and shameful treaties with tyrant enemies will also be remembered; so as not to be repeated. The optimistic Hmong spirit and exceptional success in the USA should be an encouragement to all refugees displaced by war. Assimilation in new lands is possible without losing cultural values and their strong family structure.

LS 36 mortar Hmong 1970, Garrity collection

References:

Low and Slow website table of contents:
https://www.wep11345.com/book--low-and-slow-.html

Maps:
https://www.wep11345.com/maps.html

Ray de Arrigunaga's "LAOS, The Secret War."

Part 1 Air Commando Journal Vol 3 Issue 1 pg 23

Part 2 Air Commando Journal Vol 3 Issue 3 pg 9

Part 3 Air Commando Journal Vol 3 Issue 4 pg 18

William E. Platt interview conducted by Maikou Xiong, Hmong TV, August 28, 2015:
https://www.youtube.com/watch?v=t8fPMalMSRA&feature=player_embedded

Raven 43 interview "Eyes of the Attack" History Channel video, Suicide Missions,
http://youtu.be/00YW1szygYc

Historical Material
http://www.t28trojanfoundation.com/secret-war-in-laos.html
http://www.t28trojanfoundation.com/vang-pao.html
http://www.t28trojanfoundation.com/will-platt.html
http://content.time.com/time/specials/packages/article/0,28804,2101745_2102136_2102247,00.html

Be well Good reader!

Thank You

About the Author

https://www.wep11345.com/about-the-author-1.html

Father, forgive them; for they know not what they do;

William E. Platt, Lt. Col. USAF Ret.

I was born in Philadelphia, Pennsylvania, the city of Brotherly Love, on 13 January 1945. It was a good year.

Fletcher N. Platt Sr., my Dad, was an aeronautical engineer during the Second World War. His brother Blaine was a US Army airborne artillery spotter in WWll's battle of the bulge. My great Grandfather Lewis McMakin was a Union cavalry officer during the Civil War. When duty called, our family volunteered to serve as citizen soldiers.

My father will always be my hero. After WWll, Dad worked for Ford motor company at the headquarters in Dearborn Michigan. As the Director of Traffic Safety and Highway Improvement at Ford, he brought his aviation experience to the automobile industry. While company vice presidents pushed for more horsepower and speed, Dad encouraged the company leaders to incorporate safety issues into the design of Ford vehicles. Seat belts, padded dashboards, collapsible steering columns and crash testing first appeared too expensive and unappealing to the Ford staff and the public. Dad's persuasive, courteous, kind and polite manner won many friends and altered the dynamics of Traffic safety products. The auto industry began to advertise safety features along with horsepower and speed. America was killing more than 50,000 citizens per year in traffic accidents. The introduction of priority engineering safety design features saved countless lives and became the industry standard by the early 1970s.

Highway design did not prioritize state of the art safety considerations. That needed to change. Dad represented the auto industry as a member of our National Transportation Safety Board. They developed high standards for the new Interstate Highway system that would span the country in asphalt and cement. Safer roads and vehicles contributed to major declines in traffic death world wide as safety awareness developed. Dad was instrumental in the education and training of the auto industry and political leaders on Highway safety issues. He testified before Congress to encourage regulations to save lives. As president of Ford at the time, family friend Robert McNamara got the credit for the safer Ford vehicles. Dad was a team player and was pleased that the automobile culture adopted and promoted auto safety improvements. He was a skilled people person who gently and effectively persuaded decision-makers to do the right thing for customers before the safety products and standards were profitable.

Dad loved to share airplane stories. In grammar school, he assembled airplane scrapbooks. Those books were in our attic with newspaper images of WW l aircraft and flight tales of daring-do. I would read aviation stories for hours and dream of low and slow flights over beautiful countryside.

My Father was also a light airplane and glider pilot. A flight with him was always a joyful experience. We rented Cessna 172 aircraft at Ann Arbor Municipal Airport. I logged over 30 hours with him before I was 13. Dad was a great instructor and gave me the yoke often. I was hooked. Hand-line control, model combat aircraft soon became a passion. I constructed and crashed several balsa wood, silk, and dope winged Fox .035 powered models. In the combat ring, I was successful in cutting off the red or blue 6-foot crate paper streamer darting from the tail of my competitions model aircraft.

Dad taught me situational awareness as we often volunteered to search the farmlands of southern Michigan for lost radio-controlled model planes. They simply flew out of range and disappeared over the horizon. Searching for these lost and wandering model aircraft from 800 feet was much fun. We located many and were heroes to the radio control pilots who recovered their expensive hobby aircraft. Those were good times, and aviation was one of my few real interests other than happy, fun, adventuresome, girlfriends.

After bicycles, my transport was a Lambretta 150 cc motor scooter, and then an elder English Ford automobile. Dad taught me how to sail and race our 16 ft. Rebel sailboats in a one-design fleet on Portage Lake. I learned to be one with the wind and knew that somehow, my life would be in the air or on the water and my windows would be open.

I graduated high school in 1963. The Vietnam War was building up quickly, and high school friends who were not going to college were immediately drafted into the US Army as privates and North Vietnamese Army (NVA) cannon fodder. Off to war, they went; not to return unbroken.

During the summer of 1964, I ventured to Europe, bought a used BSA 650cc motorcycle, and traveled through 15 countries visiting breweries, vineyards, and art history museums along my spontaneous trail of eye candy vistas and pretty girls. In Germany, I visited the Auschwitz concentration camp and realized the brutality of racial hatred, and inhumanity. West Berlin still had scars from WWll bombardment and Check Point Charlie's passage into Communist East Berlin opened my eyes to the oppression of Soviet Union communism. Walking down the drab streets there, I noticed that no one looked others in the eyes or acknowledged their presence. No smiles, no nods of good will toward a visitor. I got the message, people were fearful. They were humans without trust, surviving in submission, and living under harsh rule by tyrants. Hundreds of East Germans died attempting to escape the horrors of the communist party's manifesto. Freedom was not free in East Germany.

Many friends opted to enter the Air Force, Navy, Marines, or Coast Guard enlisted services. Other friends received marriage deferments, or medical waivers, for disqualifying ailments, habitual drug use, or queerness. Conscientious Objectors were exempt from military service, and some joined the Peace Corps service in South America. Several schoolmates skedaddled to Canada and hoped for a pardon when the war was over.

I was destined to become a passionate propeller head. In My first year at the University of Michigan, I sat for the Air Force aptitude and skills exam. Fortunately, I scored well for Pilot and Officer Training. I was in Business School, bored, struggling to concentrate, and holding down two part-time jobs as a gas station attendant and college bar bouncer. Finally, I graduated and vowed marriage to a newly graduated psychiatric RN. I was an uncooperative patient with denial issues. Flying became my priority because I was good at it.

My Basic Military Training (BMT) and Officer Training School (OTS) were at Lackland AFB, TX. My year of Flight School flew by in the border town of Laredo Texas heat. I selected the O-1 Bird Dog FAC assignment knowing that I was now in the pipeline to war in Vietnam. Water, and winter, survival schools were classic boy in the woods adventure. I studied Counter Insurgency (COIN) academics and flew my initial O-1Bird-dog qualification at Hurlburt and Holley Fields, Fl. Then I was off to Vietnam and war. I said good-bye to family and friends in June 1969.

Today hundreds of thousands of Hmong Americans continue their quest for equality, opportunity, and freedom here in the USA. Their contribution to our cultural matrix strengthens our family values and intellectual perspective. Our histories merged in 1961. Today, America is enriched by the strong adaptive goodwill of surviving Hmong war refugees and their Ameri-Hmong descendants. The refugee escape from communism and oppression is one positive results of the secret war in Laos. Their freedom is a worthy prize.

For me, there is only one race, and that is the human race. We have differences but
One-sixteenth of an inch below the surface of our skin, we are all pink!
My family supports good character, not incidental color, race, or religion.
We Love God, and we Love our neighbors. We forgive brutality as best we can. In an unnecessary war, I witnessed great suffering. I learned that love and compassion are the paths to understanding. A cheerful, peaceful life is now my priority.

Greater love hath no man than this, that a man lay down his life for his friends.

"Arlington" N. Platt collection

O1, Headed Home, Greven collection

"Taps"

Day is done, gone the sun
From the lakes, from the hills, from the sky
All is well, safely rest
God is nigh.

Fading light dims the sight
And a star gems the sky, gleaming bright
From afar, drawing near
Falls the night.

Thanks and praise for our days
Neath the sun, 'neath the stars,' 'neath the sky.'
As we go, this we know
God is nigh.

By: Horace L. Trim

Made in the USA
Coppell, TX
19 August 2024